A BEDFULL
OF FOREIGNERS

A Comedy

by

DAVE FREEMAN

SAMUEL FRENCH

LONDON
NEW YORK   TORONTO   SYDNEY   HOLLYWOOD

A BEDFULL OF FOREIGNERS

First presented by Paul Elliott and Duncan C. Weldon
for Triumph Theatre Productions on February 19th,
1974, at the Ashcroft Theatre, Croydon, with the following cast of characters:

Karak	Richard Marner
Heinz	Colin Jeavons
Stanley Parker	Terry Scott
Brenda Parker	Carole Turner
Helga Philby	Anna Dawson
Claude Philby	Tim Barrett
Simone	Lynda Baron

The Play was directed by Roger Redfarn
Designed by Terry Parsons

Subsequently presented at The Victoria Palace, London,
on April 8th, 1976, by Duncan C. Weldon, Louis I.
Michaels, Brian Rix and Peter Toerien, with the
following cast:

Karak	Peter Bland
Heinz	Colin Jeavons
Stanley Parker	Terry Scott
Brenda Parker	Julia Sutton
Helga Philby	June Whitfield
Claude Philby	Dennis Ramsden
Simone	Lynda Baron

The Play directed by Roger Redfarn
Setting by Terry Parsons

The action takes place in a bedroom in a French Hotel
near the German border

ACT I   After 9 p.m. on an evening in late October
ACT II Five minutes later

Time—the present

ACT I*

A bedroom in a French hotel in a village near the German frontier. Just after 9 p.m. on an evening in late October

The room is very old, but most of its period charm, together with its period defects, have been hidden by generations of enthusiastic paper-hangers. A few period features remain. The entrance is in the back wall. There are two other doors to the room. One leads to the bathroom; the other has been heavily disguised with wallpaper and leads to the adjoining hotel room. Above the bathroom door is a built-in wardrobe. There is also a dressing-table with a telephone on it. There are two double beds. Bed One is against the back wall, and to one side of it is the second period feature: a bay window —and across the top of the bay an elaborate old carved beam with wooden brackets. On the other side of the window is Bed Two, set against an angled wall which has a window in it above the bed. The area around Bed Two can form a separate bedroom when a folding partition is pulled out from the wall. The partition has a door in it. During Act I this remains folded up against the wall. By the side of Bed One, under the window, is an old-fashioned radiator. (See the plan of the set and Furniture and Property List on page 82)

The CURTAIN *rises on an empty stage. After a few moments Karak, the Head Porter, enters from the hallway. He is a tough, craggy man in his mid-fifties and speaks with a Slav accent. He has a dead-pan mocking sense of humour. He has a tool-bag with him, and goes to the bed lamp which is fixed to the wall above Bed One. He unplugs it and then goes to the foot of the bed and examines the lamp fitting. He takes a screwdriver from his tool-bag, looks at it, then throws it over his shoulder. He takes a second screwdriver from the bag, looks at it, and throws it over his shoulder. Finally, he takes a can of beer from the bag, looks at it, and throws the lamp fitting over his shoulder. He opens the beer can and takes a long swig*

The telephone rings. Karak goes to answer it, taking his beer can with him

Karak (*on the phone*) Hotel Heinz. . . . Oui, monsieur, we have one room left. . . . Ja, is room mit bath. . . . Ja, bathroom is working. . . . No, is not bunged up. . . . Look, why are you asking? . . . Oh, you have stayed here before. . . . No, bath is O.K. now. . . . Bath is working. Listen. (*He takes a swig from the beer and gurgles with it*) Is water going down plug-hole. . . . You are happy? Good. I am saving room for you. . . . Au revoir, monsieur. (*He hangs up and goes to the bed*) Englishman—is always worrying about bathroom—then is washing his feet in der bidet. (*He sits on the end of the bed again and takes a swig of beer*)

---

*N.B. Paragraph 3 on page ii of this Acting Edition regarding photocopying and video-recording should be carefully read.

The door opens and Heinz, the Hotel Manager, enters. He is in his thirties. Slim, good looking and inept. He has a slight German accent. He carries a small poster advertising the village festival. He stands for a moment watching Karak swilling beer with an expression of disgust

Heinz (*sarcastically*) Oh, that's marvellous.

Karak chooses to misunderstand him and looks at the beer can

Karak Ja. Is not bad.

Heinz The hotel full the village festival, an important guest arriving, the entire staff run off their feet, but not you, Karak. Oh no. You are upstairs drinking.

Karak (*reasonably*) You want me *downstairs* drinking?

Heinz I don't want you drinking anywhere. (*He goes to the partition*) I want you working.

Karak So I am working. I am mending bed light.

Heinz Then hurry up and finish it. (*He hangs the poster on the wardrobe door*) I have just received a telegram. Mrs Hoffmeyer is arriving.

Karak Mrs Hoffmeyer?

Heinz Yes, Karak, Mrs Hoffmeyer.

Karak So who in hell is Mrs Hoffmeyer?

Heinz The President of the Bulgarian Ladies' Cycling Club.

Karak Oh? Is good, ja?

Heinz I am trying to get the hotel placed on their approved list. It's very, very important for us. Their standards are extremely high. The least thing wrong, the tiniest complaint—and you are struck off their list for ever.

Karak continues to swig beer

Karak So where are you sticking her?

Heinz I am *accommodating* her in that room next door, and, Karak, I want everything in that room working properly. I want everything perfect.

Karak So how can room be perfect when hotel is falling to bits?

Heinz Oh, don't talk rubbish.

Karak Is falling to bits I'm telling you. Is all rotting and full of woodworm.

A cuckoo clock on the wall cuckoos. Heinz looks at his watch

Heinz (*accusingly*) That clock is slow.

Karak Ja. Woodworm is attacking cuckoo.

Heinz Impossible.

Karak Why is impossible?

Heinz Because, Karak, that cuckoo is plastic, and woodworm do not eat plastic.

The radiator gives three sharp bangs

What's that?

Karak (*sepulchrally*) Is death watch beetle.

The radiator bangs again

Heinz It's that radiator. I thought the plumber came to look at it?

Karak Oh ja, plumber is looking at it, and plumber is recommending you buy new one.

Heina (*shocked*) A new *radiator*?

Karak A new hotel.

Heinz Oh, very funny. Well I am not concerned with what the plumber thinks, but I am concerned with Mrs Hoffmeyer, and it's very important *she* finds nothing wrong.

Karak Ja.

Heinz Furthermore, I mentioned in my letter, that *here* we speak Bulgarian.

Karak Oh, is good. I didn't know you are speaking Bulgarian.

Heinz Not me, you idiot. *You!*

Karak *Me?*

Heinz You told me once you were Bulgarian.

Karak No—I told you I was Hungarian.

Heinz Oh, so *now* you are a Hungarian?

Karak No, is just what I am telling you.

Heinz Then where the hell *are* you from?

Karak I am coming here from Foreign Legion. Legion is giving me pension, and making me French citizen.

Heinz Yes, but what were you before you *joined*?

Karak Oh, before that I was a foreigner. You see to get in legion you *have* to be a foreigner. If you are not foreigner, they don't bloody want you.

Heinz Well *I* don't want you, either.

Karak Ah, but you are inheriting me along mit hotel. Your aunt said I was to be kept in job as concierge as long as I am wishing.

Heinz Well don't push me too far, Karak. I can take it to court. I can fight the will.

Karak Oh, you can fight, but you are not winning. You see here you are foreigner. You are some sort of Swiss-Austrian. (*With mock, humorous grandeur*) Whereas *I* am former soldier of France.

Heinz Look, I have no time to argue with you. The moment you have finished up here go down and relieve Marcel at reception.

Karak Marcel is not down there.

Heinz Well he should be down there. Where is he?

Karak He is up in his room being sick.

Heinz Sick?

Karak Ja. Is something he is eating in restaurant.

Heinz (*in alarm*) Our restaurant?

Karak Ja.

Heinz What did he eat?

Karak Chef's special. Same as guests.

Heinz Same as guests . . . Oh my God. Who's down at reception? (*He runs to the phone*)

Karak Nobody. I am putting outside calls to telephone up here.

Heinz starts dialling

What are you doing?

Heinz Phoning for an ambulance. Don't you realize, Karak. Everybody who ate the Chef's special could be sick. The entire hotel .

As Heinz is speaking on the phone Karak stands nearby talking over him

(*Into the phone*) Allo? Ici Hotel Heinz. . . . Nous avons empoissonment dans l'hôtel. . . .

Karak In that case you are needing more than one ambulance. You are needing perhaps four ambulances. Maybe six ambulances.

Heinz (*to Karak*) Will you shut up? (*Into the phone*) Ah pas vous, monsieur. . . . Non. . . . Ah bon. . . . Merci, monsieur. Au revoir. (*He hangs up and turns to Karak*) Nobody must know about this. If Mrs Hoffmeyer finds out, we are finished.

Karak O.K. (*Moving to the wallpapered door*) So I am going now to her room to check lights.

Heinz Well make sure you lock that door behind you.

Heinz moves towards the main door

And, Karak, see she has everything she wants.

Karak Ja. Everything she wants . . . excepting Chef's special.

Heinz now has the door open

Heinz *Quiet*, you idiot.

Heinz puts a warning finger to his mouth and exits

Karak (*shouting after him*) Don't worry—I am putting big bucket by her bed.

Karak picks up his tool-bag, goes to the wallpapered door and switches on the light at the door. There is a shower of sparks from the bed light

Ah good. Is working.

The lights go dim and then come up bright again, then go out altogether

Karak exits through the wallpapered door

The lights remain out and the room is lit from outside the window, dimly

A short pause and then we see the main door open as Brenda enters. She is an attractive girl in her early thirties. She is on a motoring holiday with her husband who has not yet appeared

Brenda has a plastic shopping-bag and a torch and we see her examine again the number on the room door. She calls back along the darkened passage

Brenda I've found the room, Stanley . . . (*She now holds the torch casually so that it illuminates her features*) Stanley . . . It's on the second floor. . . . Well, come back *down* a flight.

As Brenda comes into the room we hear the sound of Stanley and two suitcases falling down a flight of stairs. The lights come on. Brenda reacts

(*Calling*) Was that you, Stanley?

Stanley enters, limping and rubbing his leg

Are you all right?

Stanley Oh, I'm fine—I've only broken my leg. A couple of months in bed I'll be right as rain.

Brenda Any decent hotel and they'd *show* you up to your room.

Stanley Yes. Well perhaps the guide dog is having its dinner.

Brenda It's the last time *we* go motoring on the Continent.

Stanley (*wearily*) All right, love, we've been through all that. Don't start again.

Brenda (*moving to Bed One*) Well, honestly, it's been one thing after another. (*Pulling back the covers*) And I don't like the look of *this* place either.

Stanley What are you doing?

Brenda I'm seeing the sheets are clean. (*She looks puzzled*) And why's it got *two* double beds?

Stanley It's what they call a family room.

Brenda But we don't need *two* double beds.

Stanley All right, give me a hand and we'll sling one out the window. Look, Brenda, love. Just relax. We've got a *room*. Every hotel for twenty miles around is full, and *we've* got a room.

Brenda But, Stanley, there's something very odd going on here.

Stanley Odd?

Brenda Yes, odd. All that whispering and muttering downstairs, and then the lights all go out—and where's our luggage?

Stanley Ah—I'm afraid I let go of that when I fell downstairs.

Heinz appears at the main door with two suitcases

Heinz (*brightly*) Don't worry, sir. I have it.

Heinz takes the suitcases to the wardrobe

I must apologize for what happened. You see some idiot blew the fuses.

Brenda So we gathered.

Heinz You know you are very lucky in finding this room.

Stanley Well, the wife had a torch in her handbag.

Heinz No, I mean it's the last room we have left. Actually it was already booked by an Englishman but they haven't taken up their reservations.

Heinz opens one of the sliding doors of the wardrobe and puts the two suit-cases into it

Stanley Why is everywhere full up? I mean it's the end of October.

Heinz Ah, you see in France it's a public holiday and in this village we have the Festival of Saint Wolfgang.

Heinz points to the poster and Stanley goes to look at it

Stanley Oh, Saint Wolfgang?

Heinz Yes, it's quite a local occasion. Yes, there will be parades and fire-works and—all kinds of celebrations.

Heinz tries to shut the wardrobe door, but it has jammed. He gives a nervous laugh to Stanley

We have a little bother with this door—but it's nothing.

The siren of a French ambulance is heard approaching. Heinz panics

Oh my God—they are here. (*With a sudden burst of energy he closes the sliding-door and gets his jacket trapped in it*)

Stanley Who is?

Heinz Nobody. I seem to be trapped. I wonder could you help me?

Stanley tries to open the wardrobe door and free him. Brenda goes to the window, opens it and looks out

Brenda There's an ambulance stopped outside.

Heinz Yes, I must go.

Heinz gets out of his jacket and leaves it trapped in the wardrobe door as the sound of a second ambulance is heard

Brenda Here's another one. (*She leans out of the window*)

Stanley Is somebody ill?

Heinz Ill? Oh, good heavens no. No, it's all part of the festival. We have a—a Grand Parade—and the ambulances take part. (*He goes to the main door*)

Stanley Oh, I see.

Heinz By the way, have you had your dinner?

Stanley Yes, we ate on the way.

Heinz Thank God for that.

Heinz exits

Stanley takes off his car coat and throws it over the bed. Then he picks up the carrier-bag, goes to the pouffe and sits on it. As he speaks he takes a pair of slippers from the bag and removing his shoes puts on the slippers

Stanley You know, if it's a public holiday, we might have a job getting a room tomorrow night as well.

Brenda turns from the window

Brenda Not in here we won't.
Stanley Why?
Brenda They've just carried six people out on stretchers.
Stanley Have they?
Brenda And *that's* only the one ambulance. (*She leans out again*)
Stanley Well I never. I wonder how many they hold?
Brenda Stanley. They've just filled up two ambulances. They have taken ten people out of here on *stretchers*.
Stanley Is that the lot then?
Brenda Yes.
Stanley Well shut the bloody window. It's freezing.

The ambulances' sirens start up again as Brenda slams the window shut

Brenda Well, I'm glad you're not worried.
Stanley No. I'm not worried.
Brenda Hordes of people struck down with some unknown disease, and you are not in the least bit concerned. No, you just sit there.
Stanley You don't listen, do you?
Brenda *I* don't listen?
Stanley It's all part of the festival. Had you listened you would have heard that those two ambulances are taking part in the Grand Parade. Those people are just pretending to be ill.
Brenda Pretending? They weren't pretending. You didn't see them, did you . . . ?
Stanley Well no, but . . .
Brenda One man was yelling his head off and two of the others were groaning. Those people aren't pretending. Those people are *ill*.

Stanley looks slightly worried

Stanley Well, what's wrong with them?

Brenda starts taking things out of the carrier-bag

Brenda How would I know. It could be something dreadful. It could be infectious.

Brenda takes out an aerosol can

Stanley Well, the Manager told me . . .
Brenda Oh, they can tell you anything, can't they? Anyway, they'd hardly tell you the hotel was infested with bubonic plague.

Stanley digests this for a moment.

Stanley Bubonic plague?
Brenda Yes. Bubonic plague. (*And, holding the aerosol can, she starts spraying it round the room*)
Stanley Why bubonic plague?
Brenda (*spraying under the bed*) Why *not* bubonic plague?
Stanley Well—because they don't have bubonic plague in France.
Brenda (*still spraying*) How do you know?

Stanley Well, I mean—you'd hear about it.

Brenda Why should we hear about it? We've never even *been* here before.

She exits to the bathroom, to spray it

Stanley (*shouting after her*) Well, no, but—I mean—your father was French, wasn't he?

She returns from the bathroom

Brenda What's that got to do with it?

Stanley Well, I mean—surely he would have mentioned it, wouldn't he?

Brenda If he did I don't remember. Anyway, I was only six months' old when he left us.

Stanley (*reassuring himself*) No, it can't be, I mean, you'd read about it in the newspapers.

Brenda Unless of course they tried to hush it up.

Stanley Why would they want to hush it up?

Brenda Isn't it obvious? Bubonic plague at the height of the tourist season.

Stanley (*roused*) Height of the tourist season? This is *October*. I mean next week is November. In eight weeks it's going to be Christmas.

Brenda (*tight-lipped*) Well, I just hope that we're here to see it, that's all.

Stanley You were the one who wanted to come abroad, I wanted to go to Skegness, Remember?

Brenda (*attacking*) Oh yes—and whose idea was it that we came over here in October? Who said the weather would be nice and we'd have no bother getting rooms?

Stanley (*mildly*) Well we didn't, did we? Until tonight.

Brenda No, and look where we are tonight. In a refrigerated dormitory with the Black Death raging all around.

Stanley Oh, it's the Black Death now, is it?

Brenda I think we should leave.

Stanley Don't worry, any time from now the man'll be round with his horse and cart shouting "Bring out your dead". He can give us a lift.

Brenda Are we going or aren't we?

Stanley No we are not. It took us four hours to find an hotel with a vacancy, and now we've found one we're filling it. (*He picks up a magazine, goes over to Bed Two, and sits down on it*)

Brenda Germany's only a couple of miles away, there's bound to be hotels there.

Stanley The car is not insured for Germany.

Brenda Why didn't you insure it for Germany?

Stanley For the same reason I didn't insure it for Tahiti, Hong Kong, Saudi Arabia and the Solomon Islands. I had no idea we were going there.

Brenda Does it matter if we're not insured?

Stanley Does it matter? With the sort of luck we've had so far on this trip. It matters.

Brenda (*sighing*) Well, if you will go driving into ponds.

Stanley (*incensed*) I drove into that pond to avoid being rammed by a lunatic in a Mercedes, doing ninety miles an hour on the wrong side of the road.

Brenda Oh no he wasn't. You were on the wrong side of the road.

Stanley (*quietening*) Well, maybe I was. But I'm British. It takes a time to get used to right-hand driving. I mean, they should show some consideration for tourists—not mow 'em down like cattle.

Brenda He stopped and came back. He even offered to tow you out.

Stanley That was a fat lot of good. He didn't have a tow-rope, did he?

Brenda No. And neither did you.

Brenda takes a new hank of rope from the carrier-bag and throws it at him

Stanley No, but I've got one now. If we go in again, I'll tow myself out.

Brenda (*looking around*) Where's our suitcases?

Stanley He put 'em in the wardrobe.

Brenda goes to the wardrobe and looks at Heinz's coat

Brenda What's his jacket doing here?

Stanley He jammed it in, while you were hanging out the window, ambulance-spotting.

Brenda pushes the sliding-door and it opens perversely at her merest touch. The jacket falls out and she puts in on a chair

Brenda Well, just as long as you remember it was your idea we stayed here. (*She takes out a suitcase and puts it on Bed One, then she suddenly notices the wallpapered door. She points to it in horror*) Oh my God!

Stanley What's the matter now? (*He pats his chest*) Oh. My heart.

Brenda That door. (*She goes to the wallpapered door*)

Stanley What about it? It's locked.

Brenda It's covered in wallpaper.

Stanley Well, so what?

Brenda It's reminded me of something.

Stanley (*sighing*) Oh that. Don't worry, as soon as we get back I'll do the bloody bathroom out.

Brenda (*dramatically*) "So Long at the Fair."

Stanley I beg your pardon?

Brenda A film I saw. It was about a couple who stayed at an hotel in Paris. She went out for a walk and when she came back—he'd vanished.

Stanley Vanished?

Brenda And everybody in the hotel pretended they'd never even seen her before. They said she'd never even stayed there.

Stanley And had she?

Brenda Well of course she had. She even tried to show them the room that they'd had—but the door wasn't there.

Stanley Where was it?
Brenda Wallpapered over.
Stanley Well I expect they did it to save paint.
Brenda They didn't do it to save paint.
Stanley Well, why did they do it then?
Brenda Bubonic plague.
Stanley Oh, don't start that again.

Brenda walks back to her case, casually

Brenda Well, if you're not worried. I merely thought I'd mention it.
Stanley Now listen, we are not leaving this hotel and we're not going to have an argument. I'm going to have a shower and then we'll go downstairs and have a nice quiet drink.

Stanley goes to the wardrobe, opens his case on the rack and takes out a toilet case and towel

Brenda The bar's shut.
Stanley Well there's bound to be somewhere open, after all it's festival time. (*He takes off his jacket. Underneath he is wearing a polo-necked sweater*) It's none too warm in here, is it?

Brenda feels the radiator

Brenda The radiator's off.
Stanley Well I'll tell him about it when he comes back for his jacket.
Brenda Yes, and what was he doing? Going off like that in his shirt sleeves.
Stanley (*acidly*) Oh, it's obvious, isn't it? He's gone wallpapering. He's probably outside now with a bucket of paste. (*He jerks a thumb at the door as he does an impression of a sinister German*) Don't worry, Professor, the vorld shall never hear of our secret—ve shall vallpaper them in.

Heinz is standing at the main door in his shirt sleeves

Heinz (*surprised*) Wallpaper who in?
Stanley (*embarrassed*) Ah—er—we were talking about an old film we'd seen on television. She'll tell you about it.

Stanley exits to the bathroom

Brenda is left to face Heinz. He picks up his jacket

Heinz Ah yes, we are also getting some old films on television.
Brenda This one was about an English couple who stayed in Paris during the Great Exhibition.
Heinz Oh yes? (*He starts to put on his jacket*)
Brenda And the hotel had bubonic plague.
Heinz (*taken aback*) Plague?
Brenda And they covered the door with wallpaper.

Heinz Wallpaper?

Brenda The same as that door over there. And what were those ambulances?

Heinz (*embarrassed*) Yes. Well, from the cinema one gets a very false impression of life in other countries.

Brenda (*unconvinced*) Does one?

Heinz Oh yes. For example last night on television I was watching an old German musical about life in England. It was called "Rosen Von Soho".

Brenda Yes, but . . .

Heinz It was about a German fellow in London who falls in love with a beautiful flower girl—called Soho Rosie. Only she is really an English Duchess who is hiding.

Brenda Who from?

Heinz Oh, she is hiding from some millionaire who wishes to marry her.

Brenda Oh well, she would do.

Heinz (*dramatically acting out his words*) Well, the German fellow and Rosie are doing a tap-dance over the rooftops of Buckingham Palace, when the millionaire appears, maddened with jealousy, he tries to shoot them.

Brenda And does he?

Heinz (*continuing to act*) No. They fight on the top of Big Ben—and the mad millionaire falls to his death in Piccadilly Circus.

Brenda It sounds exciting.

Heinz It was rubbish.

Brenda Getting back to what we were saying . . .

Heinz On the other hand. It had some rather nice songs in it.

Brenda What was wrong with those people downstairs?

Heinz I am trying to remember how they went . . .

Brenda Oh, they went in two ambulances.

Heinz No, no. The songs in the picture. Ah yes, one of them is coming back to me. It was partly in English. (*He starts singing to Brenda with great feeling, leading her to the pouffe and seating her*)

Von ganzen die blumen in Soho
Von ganzen die Rosen on view
Of all the flowers we see on display
The Rose I love best is you . . .

Brenda (*stunned*) Oh, it's quite nice—yes.

Heinz has not finished, however, and kneels beside her

Heinz (*singing*) Rosie my Rosie
            Ich lieber dich Viel zu Viel.
    (*He sits beside her*)

Brenda Yes, well—er . . .

Heinz Yes?

Brenda Yes. You have an—er—unusual voice.

Heinz At medical school, I was in the Amateur Operatic Society.

Brenda (*surprised*) Are you a doctor?

Heinz Not—exactly. But I was a medical student for nine years.

Brenda It's a long course, isn't it?

Heinz *Not* if you can pass the exams. Of course, my aunt was supporting me, until she passed away.

Brenda Oh, I am sorry.

Heinz So am I. It means I have to run this hotel.

Brenda Yes well, of course, medical knowledge must come in very handy—especially when you have an epidemic. (*She rises*)

Heinz (*emphatically*) We do not have an epidemic. (*He leaps up*)

Brenda But those ambulances . . .

Heinz Merely a minor case of food poisoning.

Brenda Then why did you . . .

Heinz Merely a precaution. (*He leads her back to the pouffe and seats her*) You see with Mrs Hoffmeyer arriving, I thought if those people *are* going to be ill, it's much better they are ill in hospital—where she can't see them. (*He sits beside her*)

Brenda now relaxes, completely relieved

Brenda Oh, you know for a moment I was very worried.

Heinz (*ardently*) I could see you were. (*He takes her hand and gazes at her*) You know you are very lovely.

Brenda (*uneasily*) Thank you.

Heinz You remind me so much of someone I once loved.

Brenda Do I? (*She rises and moves away*) Well I'm married.

Heinz So was she. (*He follows her and takes her hand*)

Brenda My husband's with me.

Heinz So was hers.

Brenda He's right there—in the bathroom.

Heinz You are radiant, you are adorable. You are the loveliest woman I I have ever met. Am I offending you by saying all this?

Brenda No . . . Well yes, I'm married, and he could come out any second.

Heinz Then order me to leave. The moment I offend you, order me to leave. (*And he sweeps her into a passionate embrace, kissing her ardently*)

Brenda puts up a token struggle and then submits, being partly stunned by the turn of events. Heinz flings her on Bed Two and finally releases her. He turns away with a gesture of intense remorse

I am sorry. Forgive me. Such a thing will never happen again while you are under my roof. I swear it. You will never forgive me. I know this. You will never ever forgive me.

Brenda (*confused*) I'm not sure.

Heinz (*cheering up*) Well, if you should I am in room thirty-seven—along the corridor, up one flight. (*He blows her a kiss*) Auf wiedersehen—my English Rose.

Heinz exits, throwing her a rose from his buttonhole. The bathroom door opens and Stanley enters in his vest, wiping his head with a towel. He has his pullover tied round his waist, and bangs an ear with the flat of his hand

Stanley I've got water in my ears.

Brenda does not answer, she looks straight ahead still in a trance, holding the rose. Stanley bangs his ears again, and then slips his pullover on hastily

Stanley Blimey, it's freezing in here. Absolutely freezing. I've never known anything like it. It's arctic. Did you ask him?
Brenda (*absently*) Eh?
Stanley Did you ask him why the radiators weren't working?
Brenda No, I forgot.
Stanley Well that's a fat lot of good, isn't it.

Stanley goes to the radiator and turns the tap. The radiator emits a series of banging noises

That wants looking at, that does: what about those people?
Brenda People?
Stanley In the ambulances.
Brenda Oh that—that was nothing.
Stanley Nothing?
Brenda They'd just eaten something.
Stanley Oh, is that what it was. Judging by this room, I thought it might have been frostbite.
Brenda No, just a minor case of food poisoning.
Stanley Why are you using your telephone voice?
Brenda He made a pass at me.
Stanley Who did?
Brenda The Manager—well he didn't exactly make a pass at me.
Stanley Well, did he or didn't he?
Brenda He said I looked radiant. He said I was the loveliest woman they'd ever had staying here.
Stanley Did he?
Brenda Yes.
Stanley You know why he said that, don't you?
Brenda Why?
Stanley So you wouldn't ask him about that bloody radiator.
Brenda (*hurt*) Well, if that's all you think of me.
Stanley They're all the same, these foreigners. Full of chat. I mean you don't want to let it worry you.
Brenda Oh, I wasn't worried.
Stanley He didn't pinch your behind, did he?
Brenda No, he did not.
Stanley Well, that's all right then. He was just laying on the old chat . . . Ooh. (*He suddenly clasps his ear*) Oh dear, oh dear.
Brenda What's wrong?
Stanley It's this water in my ears, it keeps making whoom-whoom noises.
Brenda Well it's wax, you ought to get them syringed.
Stanley I know that, but where?
Brenda (*thoughtfully*) I suppose *he* could do it for you.
Stanley Who?

Brenda The Manager.

Stanley The Manager?!

Brenda Well he's the owner actually. His aunt left it to him.

Stanley I don't care who left it to him. I'm not having my ears messed about by hotel managers.

Brenda He's a sort of doctor—well, nearly

Stanley Nearly?

Brenda He was a medical student, I don't think he's actually practised.

Stanley Well he's not practising on me. Is there anything else he does?

Brenda Well he—sings.

Stanley Sings?

Brenda He was singing a song—out of an old silent film.

Stanley Was he? Well that couldn't have been easy for a start.

Stanley goes to the bathroom, leaves the towel, and returns

Brenda Perhaps it wasn't silent—perhaps it was an early talkie. Anyway, I am sure he *would* look at your ear.

Stanley Oh I'm quite sure he would if he got the chance, but he's not damn well going to.

Brenda How is it?

Stanley Oh, it's all right—if it goes again we'll send for him—the hotel doctor—chats up the ladies and sings while he syringes, and fleets of ambulances carry off his successful cases.

Brenda looks at her hand in horror

Brenda (*rising*) Oh no.

Stanley What?

Brenda It's gone.

Stanley What has? What?

Brenda That ring my mother gave me—I've lost it.

Stanley Well it's him. He's had it.

Brenda Who?

Stanley The Manager.

Brenda Oh, don't be so stupid.

Stanley Well of course it's him. He's had it.

Brenda Wait a minute. I'm trying to think—it was that filling station—I went to the ladies—I had a quick wash to freshen up. It took it off and put it on the shelf over the wash-basin.

Stanley But that was miles away—before we stopped for tea.

Brenda Yes but we got lost after that and went round and round in circles.

Stanley It's still about four hours away. I don't even know where it was.

Brenda Oh, I can remember—at least I think I can. (*Contritely*) Oh, I am sorry, darling. I'm such an idiot. (*She is on the verge of tears*)

Stanley Well, don't get upset. It could have happened to anybody, love.

Brenda I feel so awful.

Stanley Just don't get upset about it, love.

Brenda puts her arms round him

Brenda Oh darling, you are sweet, you really are. Most men would scream and shout, but you're taking it all so calmly.

Stanley Well, what's done is done.

Brenda Yes, but you're taking it so well, darling. I mean, just think, you've driven all this way today—and now you've got to drive all that way back. Don't worry. I'll drive part of the way.

Stanley Oh no, you won't.

Brenda Oh yes I will.

Stanley Oh no, you won't.

Brenda Why?

Stanley Because we're not bloody well going back. That's why.

Brenda Not going back?

Stanley Do you think a diamond ring left in a ladies' lavatory is still going to be there?

Brenda Yes—well it might be—anyway, we must go and *see*.

Stanley But I don't even know what route it was on. We'll get lost again.

Brenda No we won't.

Stanley Gor blimey. We got lost in broad daylight. What chance do you think we've got at night, and even if we did find it they'll be shut.

Brenda It might be an all-night garage.

Stanley Look—I'll buy you another one for Christmas.

Brenda I don't want another one—I want that one—and what is my mother going to say when I tell her I've lost it. My father gave it to her.

Stanley Don't tell her. It wasn't all that valuable, was it?

Brenda (*angrily*) You just don't care, do you?

Stanley Of course I care . . .

Brenda You don't care.

Stanley Of course I . . .

Brenda You don't care about anything.

Stanley I care . . .

Brenda (*in full flood*) You don't care that they're carrying people out on stretchers—you don't care that that Manager tried to rape me.

Stanley (*taken aback*) Tried to *what*?

Brenda (*wishing she had not said it*) You don't care that our bathroom's like a pig-sty, you won't do it up.

Stanley (*astounded*) He tried to *what*?

Brenda (*hoping frantically to get off the subject*) Well he tried to kiss me. But you don't care—You don't care about my mother's signet ring— Well I care and I'm going back for it. Even if it takes me all night.

Stanley But you just said he tried to rape you.

Brenda If you won't go back then I'll go on my own.

Stanley You said he tried to rape you.

Brenda Yes, and I wish he had. I'd probably have let him, you're mean and you're rotten and you just don't care.

Stanley Never mind about me, what did that bloody singing manager do to you?

Brenda Nothing.

Stanley You just now said he tried to rape you.

Brenda Anyway, it's none of your business.

Stanley None of my business?... You're my wife!

Brenda You don't own me. (*She opens her suitcase on the bed and throws in the few articles she took out earlier*)

Stanley Well of course I don't own you. You don't own me. But if I went around hotels singing and raping women, you'd want to know what *I* was up to.

Brenda (*coldly*) I have not the least interest in anything you care to do. Are you driving me back to that garage or not?

Stanley No, I want a full confession of your affair with that disqualified medical sex maniac.

Brenda Then I'm off. (*She picks up the suitcase and moves to the door*)

Stanley goes after her

Stanley Brenda. Put that case down.

Brenda No.

Stanley Brenda, this is more important than losing some cheap, tatty rolled-gold ring.

Brenda (*in cold fury*) Oh no—I haven't lost that. I've still got the engagement ring you bought me—And you can have that back.

She puts down her suitcase, pulls off her engagement ring and hurls it at him. He picks it up

Stanley Don't be ridiculous—you can't break off our *engagement*.

Brenda exits

We've been married for nine years. (*He goes to the open door and shouts after her*) You can't take the car. I've got the car keys. (*With a look of triumph he feels in his trouser pockets and the look of triumph fades. He feels in both his jacket pockets, then shouts*) Brenda! Come back! Brenda!

Stanley runs to the main door and exits, closing it after him. There is a moment's pause, then Helga Philby enters, followed by Karak carrying her suitcase and a vanity case. Helga is in her late twenties, slim, tall and attractive, cool and self-possessed. A former nursing sister, she speaks excellent English with a slight German accent

Karak This way, madame.

Helga Thank you.

Karak opens the end of the wardrobe which is empty and puts Helga's case on the rack at the end. Helga meanwhile looks around the room, slightly puzzled

Are you sure my husband hasn't arrived yet?

Karak Oh oui, madame. He is asking me on telephone to hold reservations

Helga But the room is so large.

Karak Ja. It's the only one we have left.

Helga Oh, I see.

Karak Anyway, you are two peoples. You are needing large room.

Helga Yes, I know, but my husband isn't expecting me.

Karak You mean you are surprising him?

Helga Well, in a way, you see I was visiting my sister in Heidelberg and my husband rang to say he was coming here on business. And this evening I suddenly thought, it's his birthday, and he will be here all on his own. So . . .

Karak You are driving up from Heidelberg.

Helga Yes. I tried to ring my husband to tell him I was coming, but it seems he had left.

Helga looks into the bathroom

Karak So, it will be a nice surprise for him, ja? And is good job we are saving you such a big room.

Helga Yes. Mind you, I'd be happier if it was not so big and slightly warmer.

Karak Wait. (*He goes over and feels the radiator*) Ach—radiators is not switched on.

Helga Oh? Why is that?

Karak Who is knowing. Whole hotel is in state of panic.

Karak feels behind the radiator and to his slight surprise finds a spanner on the windowsill

Helga So it seems. Who was that man who rushed out as I came in?

Karak is still looking at the spanner

Karak Ah, plumber is leaving.

Helga Well if he was a plumber, why was he in such a hurry? I thought the hotel was on fire.

Karak has not been listening to her properly until now. He is putting the spanner around a turncock at the base of the radiator

Karak Not yet. All we are having at moment is food poisoning.

Helga (*severely*) Food poisoning?

Karak Is nothink.

Helga On the contrary that could be extremely serious. How many people are ill in the hotel?

Karak Is nobody ill in hotel.

Helga Oh good.

Karak Is all goink to hospital.

Helga What?

Karak But is nothink wrong with them. Manager is gettink wind up. He is sendink everybody who is eatink dinner off in ambulance. He is idiot.

Helga Oh no, he's very sensible. I remember when I was nursing in England.

Karak You were nursink in England?

Helga Oh yes. I was a staff nurse.

Karak I was in hospital there durink war. And staff nurses was always bullying me.

Helga (*sternly*) That was probably for your own good. Is that radiator working?

Karak Ja, is workink now. Is only little water squirtink out hole but is not worrying you.

Helga Do you mean it's leaking?

Karak Is nothink, in one half hour room will be warm. You wait.

Helga I think I shall take a hot bath.

Karak puts the spanner on the sill

Karak You are wanting breakfast in room?

Helga Oh. No, thank you.

Karak We are doink English breakfast. Eggs, bacon, bankers.

Helga Bankers?

Karak Ja, bankers—you are English, no?

Helga No. I am German. My husband is English.

Karak Bankers is worse.

Helga Worse than what?

Karak I am speaking German now—is worse.

Helga You mean it's worse than your English?

Karak Bankers is worse in German . . .

Helga (*enlightened*) Oh, you mean *Wurst* sausage . . .

Karak Ja, sausage.

Helga Oh, *bangers*. Yes, of course, I had forgotten.

Karak You are not eating them in England now?

Helga I don't live in England now. My husband works over here.

Karak Ja, whole of Europe is full of foreigners. All livink in wronk countries.

Helga Where did you learn your English?

Karak In Foreign Legion.

Helga Really? Where were you?

Karak Stoke-on-Trent.

Helga (*surprised*) With the Foreign Legion?

Karak Ja. You know it?

Helga Not very well.

Karak Peoples is friendly but town is dirty—full of crookery.

Helga You mean criminals?

Karak No, crookery—cups and saucers . . .

Helga Oh, *crockery*. (*She goes to her suitcase and takes out a dressing-gown and toilet bag*)

Karak Is what I am sayink. But you being German you are speakink with German accent.

Helga (*drily*) Whereas you of course speak perfect English.

Karak Ja. Although I am not actually Englishman.

Helga You surprise me. What are you?

Karak Laplander.
Helga (*astonished*) A Laplander?
Karak Ja, but reindeer is all dyink, so I am going to Foreign Legion.
Helga (*believing him*) Oh—that's very sad.
Karak Ja. Is anythink else you are wantink?
Helga No thank you. And, here's something for you.

Helga takes a coin from her handbag and gives it to him. Karak shakes her hand and salutes

Karak Merci bien, madame, danke schoen, tusand tack tack so mycket.

Karak exits

Helga You're welcome. Let's hope the water is hot.

Helga hangs her top coat, which is of a distinctive colour, in the wardrobe. Taking the dressing-gown and toilet bag, she closes the wardrobe door

Helga exits to the bathroom, slamming the door. On the slam, Heinz enters through the main door at a rush, followed by a furious Stanley

Stanley (*grimly*) A full explanation. That's what I want.
Heinz And you shall have one, sir—but not in the corridor if you please. Mrs Hoffmeyer has just arrived.
Stanley Never mind Mrs Hoffmeyer, what about my wife?
Heinz A complete misunderstanding, sir, on her part I assure you.
Stanley I hope so, for your sake.
Heinz Oh, but it was, we were discussing films, you see, especially "Rosen Von Soho".
Stanley (*puzzled*) "Rosen Von Soho?"
Heinz Also a rather unusual film your wife saw—about an exhibition in Paris.
Stanley (*shocked*) My wife doesn't watch films like that.
Heinz Oh no no. You were watching it, too. On television. You were discussing it when I came in. About wallpapering a door.
Stanley (*slightly guiltily*) Oh, that one. Yes.

Stanley moves to the armchair and sits

Heinz And then I went on to discuss an old German film, where the German man falls in love with the English girl.
Stanley And she thought you were making love to her?
Heinz (*enthusiastically*) Exactly, that is absolutely correct—that is precisely what happened.
Stanley Is that the best explanation you have?
Heinz For the moment—yes.
Stanley I see. (*He rises and goes to the window*)
Heinz You are satisfied?
Stanley Not completely, no. (*He feels the radiator*)

Heinz Well, I am sorry. If you are unhappy all I can suggest is—you leave the hotel.

Stanley I should very much like to I assure you.

Heinz There will be absolutely no charge.

Stanley What for? (*He turns from the window and faces Heinz*)

Heinz For anything.

Stanley I haven't had anything. (*Darkly*) I am not sure about you, though.

Heinz But I am not *charging* you anything.

Stanley I should bloody well hope not.

Heinz So you wish to leave?

Stanley No, I can't, my wife has driven off and left me here.

Heinz Where has she gone?

Stanley To a ladies' lavatory four hours away.

Heinz But that's ridiculous. We have plenty in the hotel.

Stanley To find a ring.

Heinz Well I'm quite happy to drop the matter if you are.

Stanley For the moment, yes. We may well take it up again when she returns. *If* she returns.

Stanley sits on Bed One by the radiator

Heinz Is there anything else I can do for you?

Stanley gets up off the bed and feels the seat of his trousers

Stanley My trousers are wet.

Heinz Your *trousers* are wet?

Stanley Soaking. (*He feels the bed*) The bed's wet, too.

Heinz (*after a pause*) What have you done?

Stanley Feel that bed.

Heinz feels the bed

Heinz Oh ja, ja—somebody is wetting it. Maybe it was Karak, the Head Porter.

Stanley You mean he's been sleeping up here?

Heinz No, no. No, but he is a lunatic. He might have been throwing water over it—or something.

Stanley Well let's hope it was water.

Heinz (*going to the phone*) Don't worry, I'll call the chambermaid, oh lieber gott, I forgot she went to bed early . . . Never mind, I will get her up. (*On the phone*) Give me Madelaine. (*Without waiting for a reply he takes the earpiece away and speaks to Stanley*) We are so short of staff you see, and I have to get changed for my part in the festival. (*Into the phone*) Allo? . . . Madelaine, venez a la chambre douze, vit s'il vous plait. Le couverture est mouille—le lit est mouille. . . . Toute suite. . . . Bon. (*He hangs up*) She is half asleep I think, but don't worry, the chambermaid will be down instantly—in five seconds.

Heinz exits

Stanley meanwhile tries to find the source of the damp bed. He looks around and sees the radiator; he feels it and discovers the leak. Then he picks the spanner up and turns off the cock at the bottom. As he does so the radiator emits a series of loud bangs and a rush of steam. Stanley looks at it and shakes his head, and then, still carrying the spanner, he goes to the main door, opens it and shouts down the corridor after Heinz

Stanley The radiator is leaking—the radiator is leaking.

Obviously Stanley has just missed Heinz so he exits after him. After a moment Helga comes out of the bathroom carrying her clothes and wearing her dressing-gown

She goes to the wardrobe and hangs up her clothes. The door gives no trouble. She shuts the wardrobe, which now contains all her clothes except the dressing-gown she is wearing. She goes over to the radiator and fiddles with the top. Then she holds her hand a little way away, obviously feeling a fine jet of water coming out. She looks at the bed and feels it

Helga Oh. What an hotel. (*She pulls back the cover and feels the mattress*)

Stanley enters with the spanner. He calls back down the passage as he enters

Stanley And don't forget the chambermaid.

Stanley sees Helga. He thinks she is the chambermaid. She thinks he is the plumber

Stanley Ah, good evening.
Helga Oh, good evening. It's the radiator.

Stanley goes to the radiator

Stanley Yes, I know. Yes, I'm sorry if we've got you out of bed.
Helga No, I wasn't in bed. I was taking a shower.
Stanley Oh, were you?
Helga Yes. Mind you I could have taken one standing here, from the radiator.
Stanley Well there's no point in you standing there getting wet. Move out of the way, perhaps I can do something.
Helga I certainly hope so.

She goes over and sits on Bed Two and watches him, as he tries to shut off the water at the bottom cock. Stanley feels somewhat guilty about bringing the chambermaid out of her shower and his manner is slightly apologetic. He takes her somewhat reproving attitude to be a natural resentment at being brought down. Helga wants him to hurry up and leave

Stanley Yes, well it's a very old radiator.
Helga Yes, like everything else in this place.
Stanley Yes.

Helga Where were you running to earlier on?
Stanley Running to?
Helga Yes. You nearly knocked me over.
Stanley Did I? I'm sorry, I didn't see you. I was in a bit of a hurry.
Helga Yes, you were. (*She sits sprawled out on the bed*)

Stanley makes the radiator bang a couple of times and then stands up

Stanley If you turn it one way it leaks, if you turn it the other way it
   bangs.
Helga Well, we can't have banging all night, can we?
Stanley No . . . (*He gives her a puzzled look*) It'll just have to leak, then.
Helga All right, so let it.
Stanley Well there's not much point in changing the sheets, then.
Helga No, not really.
Stanley So that's it, then.

*He expects Helga to get up and go. She is waiting for him to leave. They
look at each other slightly puzzled*

Helga Yes.
Stanley Yes.

*Helga lies on the bed, looking at him, and Stanley starts to feel uneasy.
She seems extremely forward for a chambermaid*

Helga Well, it doesn't matter. We can use this one.

*This remark confirms Stanley's growing suspicions. He still can't quite
believe his ears, however*

Stanley I beg your pardon?
Helga I said we can use this bed.
Stanley That's what I thought you said. Yes.
Helga Don't you understand what I'm saying?
Stanley (*cautiously*) I think so—yes.
Helga Good. Then what are you waiting for?
Stanley I don't know. Really.
Helga What do you mean you don't know. Have you finished fiddling
   with the radiator?
Stanley Well, yes, I think so—I mean there's not a lot I can do. (*He turns
   to the radiator again to give himself time to think*)

*Helga now leans on one elbow; she looks at him and sighs. He seems to her
a typical incompetent workman*

Helga Oh, now look, if you can't do anything, say so.

Stanley turns from the radiator at her tone of contempt. He is stung by it

Stanley (*coldly*) Oh, I wouldn't say that.
Helga Well, I would.
Stanley No, I am quite sure I could if I wanted to.
Helga But you don't *want* to? Is that what you are saying?

Stanley I'm *thinking* about it.

Helga You are *thinking* about it?

Stanley That's what I said. Yes.

Helga Oh, stop making excuses. If you *can* do it, then for heaven's sake get on with it. (*And she lies back on the bed*)

Stanley is stung beyond endurance by her manner, and her challenge to his virility

Stanley (*shouting*) Right, then. (*He starts to take off his trousers*)

Helga sits up slowly in horror

Helga (*shouting angrily*) What the hell are you doing?

Stanley What?

Stanley freezes with his trousers half off

Helga What are you doing?

Stanley I was—er—taking my trousers off.

Helga (*incredulously*) To mend the *radiator*?

Stanley No . . .

Helga Well, to what?

Stanley Well I've got wet trousers, you see. They're soaking wet—I've got wet trousers . . .

Helga Put them on again.

Stanley No, it's true. I've wet my trousers—I mean they're wet. Honestly, they're all wet.

Helga Do you want me to call the Manager?

Stanley (*alarmed*) Oh! You wouldn't, would you? No, I was just going to bed.

Helga Where?

Stanley Over here or over there, or anywhere, I mean I was going after you'd finished, or we'd finished—we hadn't started, had we . . .? Oh Gawd. (*He is now convinced he has made some dreadful error but cannot see where*)

Helga Are you mad?

Stanley No. Just confused—I'm awfully confused.

Helga Now look, I won't tell you again. Put your trousers on and get out of here.

Stanley I mean they're soaking wet. Have a feel, they're soaking—and I have got another pair in the wardrobe.

Helga looks at him wide-eyed with horror. He points to the wardrobe

Helga Another pair of what?

Stanley Trousers.

Helga And what are your trousers doing in my wardrobe?

Stanley It's my wardrobe.

Helga Now don't be ridiculous, it's my room, so how can it be your wardrobe?

Stanley (*stunned*) Your room?

Helga Yes, of course.

Stanley But it's my room. I was given this room over an hour ago.

Helga (*horrified*) What are you saying?

Stanley I think we've made an awful mistake . . .

Helga (*swallowing*) You are not the plumber?

Stanley No, and I take it you're not . . .

Helga Not what?

Stanley Well you thought this was your room?

Helga Well, yes, of course I did, at least I thought it was my husband's room.

Stanley Ah well, that explains it, doesn't it?

Helga Yes.

Stanley Yes.

Helga Well I'm most awfully sorry, whatever must you have thought of me?

Stanley Well, I thought you were the chambermaid.

Helga Lying on the bed and telling you to get on with it?

Stanley Well, I thought . . .

Helga You thought I was a tart.

Stanley zips his trousers up again hastily

Stanley (*vehemently*) Oh no no no no no. Never. No. No, goodness No. Never. No.

Stanley shakes his head vigorously and it dislodges the wax in his ears. He starts banging his ear with the flat of his hand

Helga (*smiling*) Are you sure?

Stanley Positive, absolutely positive. Ooh, my ears.

Helga What's wrong with your ears?

Stanley I've got water in my ears. I should never have shaken my head like that.

Helga Do you know that is caused by excess wax?

Stanley Yes, I know that. Yes.

Helga And the cold makes it worse usually.

Stanley I didn't know that, actually.

Helga Take your trousers off.

Stanley Oh, not again, thank you.

Helga They're soaking wet. So take them off.

Stanley I will when you've left the room.

Helga Oh, don't worry about me. I was a nurse.

Stanley Oh well, if you advise it on medical grounds.

Stanley goes to the wardrobe and modestly turns his back to Helga as he slips his trousers down, the cuckoo clock gives a loud cuckoo. Stanley pulls his trousers up again and turns

I beg your pardon.

He realizes it was the cuckoo and slips his trousers off and Helga takes them

Helga I'll hang them up in the bathroom for you. It's a little bit warmer in there.

She goes to the bathroom

(*From inside the bathroom*) Then I must get dressed and find my husband's room.

Stanley tries to open the wardrobe. It has jammed again. He tries both ends, banging and thumping it

Helga comes back out of the bathroom

What's wrong?
Stanley It's jammed.
Helga Oh well, try the other end.
Stanley No, it's jammed both ends.

Helga tries the other end. But both doors are firmly jammed

Helga We have to open it. My clothes are in there.
Stanley You see sometimes it opens, sometimes it doesn't . . . My wife touches it and it flies open. (*He crosses to Bed Two and sits at the foot of it*)
Helga You have a wife?
Stanley Yes, of course I have.
Helga (*with slight alarm*) Well where is she?
Stanley Oh, she's just popped out for a minute.
Helga And supposing she just pops back—and finds *us* like this?
Stanley Oh no, she won't be back yet. If ever.
Helga (*sympathetically*) Ah, do you mean she has left you?

Helga sits beside Stanley on Bed Two

Stanley Oh no. Not really. No.
Helga Oh—well if you don't want to talk about it . . .
Stanley Oh no. It's just that we had a few words and she drove off and left me here—that's all.
Helga Well, don't worry.

She rests her hand reassuringly on his bare knee and he reacts

I'm sure that she will come back.

There is a loud banging on the main door. They both start

Stanley She's back!

From outside the door we hear Claude shouting angrily at Karak

Claude (*off*) Come on, man, open the blasted door.

Helga jumps up in alarm

Helga That's my husband!

Stanley follows suit

Stanley Your husband?
Helga Yes. He will kill you.
Stanley *Kill* me? Why? What do you mean, kill me? Why?

There is another loud bang on the door

Karak (*off*) Is no good banging door. You have wrong key.
Claude (*off*) Well, where's the right key?
Helga You don't know my husband.
Stanley Well—I'm getting out of here.
Helga No, don't leave me . . .
Stanley Well, you get out of here. Yes, in the bathroom. In the bathroom, quick.
Claude (*off*) Come on man.

Helga runs to the bathroom and shuts the door

Stanley sits in the armchair then realizes he has no trousers on. He gets up and runs to the bathroom door. The door opens and Helga hands him out his trousers. He struggles to put them on, stumbling across the stage as he does so

Helga (*from the bathroom*) Try to get rid of him.
Stanley Yes, I will. I'll just get my trousers on.

Helga shuts the bathroom door

Claude (*off*) Come on, man, what the hell are you doing?
Karak (*off*) I am looking for pass key.

The door opens and Claude Philby enters. He is a middle-aged and pompous English businessman. He reacts at the sight of Stanley struggling to get into his trousers. Karak follows him with a hold-all, and Claude's suit in a plastic cover

Claude (*to Karak*) Who the hell is that?
Karak Is man taking trousers off.
Stanley I am not taking them off. I am trying to put them on again.
Claude Oh, you're English?
Stanley Yes, I am English, and would you mind telling me what you are doing, bursting into my room like this?
Claude *Your* room? My dear chap, I do apologize, only this drunken fool said it was my room.

Karak puts Claude's bags down

Karak Drunk? Who is drunk?
Claude You are.
Karak So now you are insulting me. Because I am porter you think you can insult me. (*He moves towards Claude, menacingly*) Well, I am showing you different.

Karak raises a clenched fist. Claude moves behind Stanley, who is pulling on his trousers. He lays a hand on Stanley's shoulder

Claude Now that's enough of that.

Stanley moves away with alacrity

Stanley And that's enough of that as well.
Karak (*loudly*) First you are bullying me. Now you are insulting me.

Claude tries conciliatory measures

Claude All right, now calm down, there's no need for any of this. I know you have a difficult job to do.
Karak Then why are you bullying me? All the way upstairs you are shouting and bullying. Room is too expensive. Why is restaurant shut? Why is bar not open? Where is lavatory?
Claude That was not bullying. Merely a request for very urgent information.
Karak Also you are saying is lousy, rotten hotel.
Claude Merely a figure of speech.
Karak I *know* is lousy, rotten hotel, but is not my fault. Is only *me* holding it together.
Stanley Well, the radiator's leaking.
Karak Is only leaking tiny bit.
Stanley It's leaking rather a lot.

Karak goes to look at the radiator. Stanley watches him. Karak puts some chewing-gum in his mouth and starts chewing it

Claude Excuse me. Where is the lavatory?
Stanley (*unthinkingly*) Over there. (*He points to the bathroom door*)

Claude starts to move to the bathroom and Stanley, in a panic, runs to intercept him. They meet at the bathroom door

No, wait—you can't go in there.
Karak Is not your room, is this man's room. You are in wrong room.
Stanley Oh no I'm not.
Claude Look, we'll sort it out in a moment, I just want to pop in for a . . .
Stanley No.
Claude You don't mind if I just . . .
Stanley Yes.
Claude I only want to spend a . . .
Stanley I'm sorry, but not in there.
Claude Well where else can I go?
Stanley Ask him.
Claude I've already asked him—and look at him, bursting a blood vessel.
Karak (*at the radiator*) Who is bursting?
Claude I bloody well am.

Karak takes a wad of chewing-gum from his mouth and sticks it on the radiator

Karak Is good. I am stopping leak with chewing-gum.

Claude Well *I'm* not. Now look, as one Englishman to another, is it too much to ask . . .

Stanley I'm terribly sorry, but I have rather a peculiar thing.

Stanley leads Claude towards the pouffe

Claude Oh, have you?

Stanley About sharing lavatories.

Claude I don't want to share it. I want to borrow it. When I've finished you can have it back.

Claude makes a run at the bathroom door and turns the handle. He gives a cry of frustration. Stanley follows him over

It's locked.

Stanley Well of course it's locked—my—er—my wife is in there taking a bath.

Claude Well why the hell didn't you say so before?

Stanley Now listen, I was given this room over an hour ago.

Karak Who is giving you?

Stanley The Manager.

Karak (*with scorn*) Manager is idiot. Is always making mistakes.

Claude There, you see . . .

Stanley Well I'm not making one.

Claude You are if you argue with him.

Karak Is no mistake. Is that gentleman's room.

Claude Right, that settles it. Now will you kindly get your wife out of my bathroom?

Stanley No.

Claude Very well then. Open the door and let me in.

Stanley She is having a bath.

Claude All right then. Blindfold me.

Stanley You're disgusting.

Claude I shall be even more disgusting if I don't get in there. I give you thirty seconds to get your wife out of my bathroom.

Stanley Thirty seconds?

Claude It's not very much, but it's all I can manage. I am a desperate man.

Stanley (*to Karak*) Can't you find him another one?

Karak Certainly—if he is nice to me. (*He mimes money by rubbing his finger and thumb*)

Claude Yes, I'll be nice to you—I apologize for everything—I'd go on my knees if I could. What more can I do?

Stanley Try a drink?

Claude (*aghast*) *What!!?*

Stanley Not for you, for *him*.

Claude (*fishing out change*) Here you are, here's a franc . . . two francs.

He proffers the notes to Karak, who regards them with contempt

Three? . . . All right, *five*. Five francs—beyond that I will not go. Well
I will go—but it won't be in the . . .

Karak (*taking the money*) O.K., follow me.

Karak exits

Claude Thank you. (*He follows Karak to the door and turns for a parting
shot at Stanley*) And you be out of here when I return or I'll have you
forcibly ejected.

Claude exits hastily after Karak

*Stanley tries the wardrobe again, then runs to the bathroom and knocks on
the door*

Stanley Hey misses—madame—fraulein . . .

Helga emerges

Helga Did you get the wardrobe open?

Stanley You can see I didn't.

*They both attack the sliding doors but no amount of banging and tugging
will shift them*

Stanley It's no good, you'll have to go as you are.

Helga Yes, all right.

Stanley Well, come on—off you go.

Helga Go? Go where?

Stanley Wherever you like. How did you get here?

Helga I drove down from Heidelberg.

Stanley Well, drive back to Heidelberg. (*He tries to drag her to the main
door*)

Helga (*pointing to the wardrobe*) The car keys are in there.

Stanley Oh Gawd! Go in the corridor and hide—and then come back as
if you'd just got here.

Helga (*indicating her dressing-gown*) What? Like this?

Stanley (*wildly*) Yes . . . No . . . Well, tell him you were involved in some
sort of accident.

Helga In my dressing-gown?

Stanley No. Yes . . . Yes . . . Tell him you were taken to hospital after the
accident, and when you woke up you'd lost your memory—and you
walked out in your dressing-gown—and—and . . .

Helga (*coldly*) And now you are talking *rubbish*.

Stanley Yes. I am. Get back in the bathroom.

Helga Oh, what good's that?

Stanley To give me a chance to get your clothes out of the wardrobe.

Helga crosses to the wallpapered door

Helga Where does that lead?

Stanley I don't know. Anyway it's locked. Look, we haven't done anything. Why don't we just explain?

Helga To Claude? You have seen what he's like. If he comes back and finds me like this with you . . .

Stanley Yes, what have you got on underneath?

Helga Nothing.

Stanley (*screaming*) Nothing? Nothing at all?

Helga I was taking a shower.

Stanley drags Helga to the door

Stanley Oh, Gawd. Get out of here. Go out in the corridor and hide. (*He pulls open the door and peers out in the corridor. Then he comes in again rapidly and slams the door*) Too late, he's coming.

Stanley⎫
          ⎬ The bathroom. ⎰ (*Speaking together*)
Helga⎭

Stanley half drags her to the bathroom

Helga exits to the bathroom

Stanley gallops over to Bed Two, jumps on it, picks up the magazine and pretends to be reading the moment he is in position

Claude enters, carrying a lavatory chain

Claude You're still here, then?

Stanley That's obvious, isn't it?

Claude You realize you have cost me five francs and a great deal of inconvenience.

Stanley Don't tell me, complain to the Manager.

Stanley gets off the bed and feels the back of his trousers, which are obviously wet. He saunters over to the radiator and stands with his back to it

Claude What are you doing?

Stanley My trousers are wet.

Claude Well, it's no thanks to you that mine aren't. (*He unrolls the lavatory chain from around his hand*) And look at this.

Stanley What are you? Some sort of an hotel souvenir collector?

Claude At my first pull the handle came off the chain. At my second pull, the chain came off the cistern. At my third pull, the cistern came off the wall.

Stanley And what will you do with it?

Claude I haven't decided yet. I shall probably wrap it around somebody's neck and strangle them with it.

Stanley, alarmed at the threat, moves from the radiator towards Bed Two

Stanley Get away from me—you—skinhead.

Claude What?

Claude follows him and thoughtfully wraps the chain around his knuckles. He unwinds the chain and flails it around

Or I could wave it around like this. (*He flails the bed with it*)

Stanley (*picking up a chair to defend himself*) I see no need for violence.

Claude (*lashing the bed*) Don't you?

Stanley That is an offensive weapon.

Claude And it came from a very offensive place. If you don't believe me, go along and look at it. (*He flails the chain again*)

Stanley Get away. You're a maniac—get away.

Heinz enters. He is dressed in a very elaborate Renaissance costume, and carries a pike. He has a helmet which sprouts feathers in all directions

Claude looks at him in astonishment. Stanley puts the chair down

Heinz Gentlemen.

Claude Who the hell are you?

Heinz (*proudly*) I am the High Constable of France.

Claude (*pointing to Stanley*) Then arrest that man for trespass.

Heinz No, no. Merely for the pageant. Otherwise I am the Hotel Manager.

Claude finds this hard to believe. He turns to Stanley for confirmation

Claude (*pointing*) Is he the Hotel Manager?

Stanley No, he's the bird man of bloody Alcatraz.

Heinz The hall porter tells me there has been some slight confusion over the bookings.

Stanley Yes, so take him out of here and put him in a padded cell.

Heinz I'm afraid we have no padded cells in this hotel, sir.

Stanley (*bitterly*) Oh, you *must* have.

Claude Now listen. The hall porter booked me into this room.

Heinz (*aloofly*) And *I* booked this gentleman in.

Claude Then you've made a mistake, haven't you?

Heinz I am the Manager. I do not make mistakes.

Claude But the hall porter . . .

Heinz Is a lunatic. In any case, as Manager, my decision takes precedence over that of the hall porter.

Claude (*with menace*) Oh, does it?

Stanley Definitely.

Heinz Quite, quite definitely.

Claude In that case, my fine feathered friend, I shall sue you!

Heinz (*taken aback*) Sue me?

Claude And furthermore, I shall report to the police that I have been assaulted, threatened, and placed in personal jeopardy. After that I shall report you to the Chamber of Commerce, the Tourist Board, and— (*he dangles the lavatory chain*)—the local sanitary inspector!

Heinz (*shocked*) Lieber Gott!

Stanley He's bluffing you.

Claude You keep out of this.

Stanley Keep out of it? I'm the one who's been assaulted, threatened and placed in jeopardy. This man attacked me with a bicycle chain.

Heinz A bicycle chain? From whose bicycle was he taking it?

Stanley Does it matter?

Heinz Of course it matters. It might have been Mrs Hoffmeyer's.

Claude You don't peddle it, you *pull* it. It's a lavatory chain.

Heinz (*to Stanley*) There is a difference between a lavatory and a bicycle.

Stanley Well he wouldn't know so I should warn Mrs Hoffmeyer to bring hers in.

Claude And furthermore, I was not attacking him. I was merely defending myself.

Stanley You liar!

Heinz Now now, gentlemen, please—we don't want any trouble.

Claude Oh, it's a little late for that, monsieur. Do you really think you can treat a member of the British Corps Diplomatique, in this fashion? Well, do you?

Heinz (*awed*) The Corps Diplomatique? You are a British Diplomat?

Stanley He can't be. He was attacking me with that chain. Is that the action of a man responsible for—British Policy?

Claude It is the policy of Great Britain to defend herself whenever attacked.

Stanley With lavatory chains?

Claude That's about all we've got left nowadays.

Heinz Gentlemen, wait. There is a solution to all this if you are both agreeable.

Claude And what's that?

Heinz Well, this is a family room, with two large beds in it. You are two gentlemen on your own.

Stanley But I am not on my own. I have a wife, remember?

Heinz Well, yes.

Stanley You should do.

Heinz Ah, but she is not here.

Claude Yes, she is. She's in the bathroom.

Heinz You mean she has come back?

Claude Obviously.

Heinz But when did she return? I have been down in reception. I didn't see her come through.

Stanley No, she came up another way.

Heinz (*keenly*) There is no other way.

Heinz and Claude both look at Stanley, who looks guilty

Stanley Why . . . Why should I say . . . Why should I say I had a wife in the bathroom if I hadn't had a wife in the bathroom?

Heinz (*sternly*) There is a difference between having your wife and having some other woman.

Stanley Oh, is there, and how do you know? Or have you tried?

Claude Now this is quite easily settled, we just open the door and see who she is.

Heinz Yes, of course.

Stanley No.

Heinz You realize that for immoral behaviour I can ask you to leave this hotel immediately.

Stanley Immoral behaviour? Me . . .?

Heinz Yes, sir. You. (*And he bangs the pike down hard to emphasize his point*)

Stanley And what about you and the love scene from "Rosen Von Soho"?

The blow strikes home and Heinz changes his tactics

Heinz Yes. Well I am quite sure there is no woman in the bathroom.

Claude Let's go and look.

Heinz (*firmly*) No. I am quite prepared to take his word for it.

Claude He hasn't given you one.

Heinz That's good enough for me. I take it you are quite prepared to share the room. Yes?

Claude No.

Stanley Certainly not.

Claude What about the woman in the bathroom? Are we sharing her as well?

Heinz As far as I am concerned there is no woman in the bathroom.

Claude But there's *someone* in there. You try the door.

Heinz (*firmly*) No. I am the Manager, and my decision is final. There is nobody in the bathroom. (*He moves to the main door as if to exit*)

Stanley I'm not sharing with him.

Claude Nor I with him.

Heinz Well, there is one other solution to the problem. Toss up for it.

Stanley No.

Claude mulls it over a moment

Claude Yes, all right. Why not?

Stanley No.

Heinz Why not?

Stanley Because I don't wish to.

Claude Well we do, and it's two against one.

Claude takes a coin out of his pocket and hands it to Heinz, who tosses it

Heads.

Heinz (*uncovering the coin*) Oh, it's tails.

Stanley Ah, you lost.

Claude Indeed I have, and therefore, as a sportsman and a gentleman, I agree without any hesitation to share the room.

Stanley But that's not what we tossed for.

Claude Oh yes it is. You ask him.

Heinz Yes, it is. That's quite correct. The matter is now closed. In any case there is a partition you can pull out. It makes two completely separate rooms. You will have complete and utter privacy.

Heinz goes to the partition and tugs on the handle. The partition does not budge. He bangs it and finally kicks it

We are having a little bother with it. But don't worry. I'll get the hall porter.

Heinz goes to the main door and exits

Claude (*turning to Stanley*) All right, then. Now who have you got in that bathroom?

Stanley A—er—personal friend.

Claude Then get rid of her.

Stanley Well, you don't expect me to bring her out in front of you, do you?

Claude Why? I don't know her, do I?

Stanley No. No it's just—er—it might embarrass her.

Claude Well if she stays she will certainly embarrass *me*.

Stanley (*worried*) What do you mean?

Claude (*turning*) What do I mean? (*He picks up his suit*) You don't imagine I intend to share the room with you and some cheap tart you've picked up.

Stanley She is not a cheap tart.

Claude Well, of course you know what you're paying her, but let me make it quite clear. I have no desire to participate in your primitive sex orgies. (*He goes to the wardrobe*)

Stanley You haven't been invited.

Claude tries to open the wardrobe door

And you won't open that, it's jammed.

Claude presses the sliding door and it glides back effortlessly. It reveals Helga's dress and coat hanging on the rail and her suitcase in the rack. Claude, however, does not look in. He turns to Stanley still holding his suit

Claude What do you mean jammed?

Stanley is riveted with horror, and, as Claude turns once more to the wardrobe, he screams

Stanley Wait! Wait—oh—no—wait . . . No—I was thinking—supposing— (*he rushes over to Claude and puts his arm round him in a friendly gesture, stopping him from seeing into the wardrobe*)—supposing I got her to go?

Claude Yes?

Stanley Would you leave the room for ten minutes?

Claude Why ten minutes?

Stanley Well, so I can—er—say good-bye to her.

Claude You're disgusting. You're an animal. You're like some species of sexually deprived stoat.

Stanley Yes, possibly I am, but it does mean a great deal to me.

Claude I'm sure it does, but I'm not hanging about in the corridor while you have a quick . . .

Stanley How dare you!

Claude Now don't you get uppity with me.

Stanley (*humbly*) I'm sorry—sorry.

Claude Because *you* are in no position whatsoever to be offended at my remarks.

Stanley No. No, I'm not.

Claude You must be sex mad.

Stanley Yes, I am. Yes.

Claude I shall give you three minutes.

Stanley (*wailing*) Three minutes? (*He lets go of Claude in his surprise*)

Claude Long enough for a decent farewell, and too short for an indecent one.

Stanley Make it five.

Claude (*sternly*) Three. (*He turns to the wardrobe again*)

Stanley (*shouting*) No!

Stanley shouts to divert Claude's attention from the wardrobe. It succeeds to the extent that Claude hangs his suit up without noticing Helga's clothing. He turns to Stanley even as he hangs it up

Claude (*sternly*) Now look, if I have any more, I shall make it *two*. (*He starts to shut the wardrobe door*)

Stanley (*wailing*) No, don't do that.

Claude shuts the wardrobe door with a slam, he looks at Stanley in distaste as he walks to the main door

Claude You are repulsive. To a respectable man like me, you are repulsive.

Stanley (*humbly*) Thank you very much.

Claude goes to the main door and exits

Stanley runs to the wardrobe and tries to open it. It has jammed again. He kicks it in a fury

Helga comes out of the bathroom and runs over

Helga Claude *was* angry, wasn't he?

Stanley He is a pompous, arrogant pig.

Helga (*coldly*) You are referring to my husband.

Stanley Yes, I am, and if you don't hurry up he'll be back here any minute now.

They redouble their efforts to open the wardrobe

Helga I know he was angry, but that's how he is. He can't stand anything immoral. He finds anything to do with sex, distasteful.

Stanley (*irritatedly*) It must be a load of fun for you.

Helga looks at him outraged. Stanley wishes he had bitten his tongue off

Helga (*coldly*) How dare you?

Stanley I'm sorry. I didn't mean that. That was quite unforgivable of me.

Helga (*mollified*) Well I forgive you—but there are more things in life than sex, you know.

Stanley Yes. And getting you out of here is one of them. (*He heaves at the wardrobe again. He almost wails at the injustice of it*) He just touched it and it flew open. (*He gives up*) Oh, it's no good.

He stands aside wearily and Helga tries again

Helga I must get my clothes out.

Stanley It's a waste of time. Go back in the bathroom.

Helga I am not going back in that bathroom. I've already had two showers and a bath. What do you think I am—a mermaid? (*She tries the wall-papered door*)

Stanley Well you can't go in the corridor, he's out there. (*He looks over at the door and remembers*) Oh my God, I haven't even locked the door.

Stanley runs over to the door and locks it. Helga meanwhile looks round and runs over to the big window. She opens it and looks out. Stanley turns and sees her

Helga The window . . .

Stanley (*alarmed*) What about it?

Helga (*tragically*) It's the only way out.

Stanley (*running to her*) No—no—please don't jump.

Helga (*calmly*) I wasn't going to. I mean it's the only way out the room.

Stanley But we're two storeys up.

Helga We'll tie some sheets together, you can lower me out.

Stanley No, you'll kill yourself, I won't let you.

Helga Oh, don't worry about me, I've had lots of climbing experience, that's nothing. (*She whips the bedding off Bed One and starts tying two sheets together*) If we only had some rope.

Stanley Rope?

Helga Yes, rope.

Stanley I've got some rope, I bought some . . .

Stanley runs and finds his coil of rope. He hurries to the window. Helga drops the sheets and climbs on to the window-sill, using Bed One as a stepping-stone

It's a tow-rope for the car. I got it to tow us out of a pond. The whole trip's been nothing but a disaster. (*He hands Helga the rope*)

Helga Shhh! Thank you.

Helga ties one end of the rope in mountaineering fashion around her. In full command of the situation, she throws the rope over the beam above the window. Stanley, meanwhile, moves round indecisively, then runs to check the main door is locked

Stanley I wish we'd gone to Blackpool. Nothing can happen to anybody in Blackpool. Sprain your wrist on the fruit machines, that's all that can happen to anybody in Blackpool.

Stanley runs back to the window. Helga gives him the end of the rope

I'll put it round the radiator. (*He passes it through a vane of the radiator, thus ensuring a purchase*)

Helga There you are. Now you have to lower me slowly. And don't worry. I shall be perfectly all right.

Stanley turns his back to the radiator and puts the rope over his shoulder, ready to take the strain. He has last-minute doubts

Stanley Oh dear. I wish you wouldn't.

Helga (*softly*) Oh, you've been sweet—you really have.

Stanley (*surprised*) What, me?

Helga Yes. You could have walked out and left me to Claude.

Stanley No I couldn't. No.

Helga Well, if we don't meet again, thank you for everything. (*She turns him to her and kisses him*) Keep the rope taut.

Stanley Yes, right. (*He pulls and almost hauls her up with it*)

Helga Ah—not too taut—slacken it a little—that's it. (*She steps out of the window on to the outer sill*) Now lower.

Stanley Lower.

He strains at the rope over his shoulder as Helga starts to gradually go down outside the window

Helga Lower.

Stanley Lower.

Helga, outside the window, gradually goes down a short ladder and then bends her knees until she is almost out of sight. Stanley keeps up his tension on the rope

Are you all right?

Helga Yes, I'm fine—keep lowering.

Helga disappears from sight. In actuality she is now lying down on the stage but keeping the rope taut by pulling it down to her

Stanley keeps lowering the rope and then there is a sudden cry of alarm from Helga

Oh—wait!

Stanley What's the matter?

Helga (*outside*) My dressing-gown. It's caught on a hook.

Stanley (*panicking*) What shall I do?

Helga Haul me up again.

Stanley leans on the rope, but it will not move

Stanley I can't.

There is a loud banging at the main door

Claude (*off*) All right, open up! You've had your three minutes.
Stanley (*shouting*) No, wait—please—please! I must have more time.
Claude (*off*) Just stop it and let me in.
Helga (*off*) Haul me up.
Stanley (*shouting*) I can't!
Claude (*off*) Yes you can.
Stanley I can't.
Claude (*off*) Then you shouldn't have bloody well started.
Stanley Five more minutes. Please . . .
Claude (*off*) No—I'm going for the pass key.
Stanley (*to Helga*) He's going for the pass key. Oh, I knew we should have gone to Blackpool.

Stanley looks around frantically and then, still firmly grasping the rope with one hand he ties the end of the rope in a vane of the radiator. Then he runs for a chair, takes it to the door and wedges it under the door handle. Helga gives a loud scream. Stanley turns and stops, petrified in horror, as the radiator starts to go up in the window alcove. It comes to rest nearly on the ceiling. Steam spurts out from around it. Helga keeps the rope taut as the radiator goes up

Stanley (*shouting*) Are you all right?
Helga (*outside*) No—I am stark naked.
Stanley (*horrified*) *Stark naked?*

Stanley leans out the window and steam hits him in the stomach. He covers his eyes and reels back in agony

Your dressing-gown's caught on that hook.
Helga (*outside*) Well do something—haul me up or lower me down. I'm hanging here.
Stanley Yes, hang on—stay there. Stay there—hang on. Oh, how the hell did I get into this—it's all the wife's fault—that and that rotten ring. (*He jumps up and down trying to get to the rope on the radiator, but it is too high up. He goes to the door and takes the chair from under the handle, and then, puffing and panting, runs back to the window, gets on the chair and undoes the rope. Then he starts to lower the rope again*)
Helga (*off*) Please hurry.
Stanley (*groaning*) Slowly—slowly—slowly . . . Are you down?
Helga (*off*) Yes, but I can't stop—somebody's coming.

Stanley strips off his jumper and trousers and throws them out of the window

Stanley Wait a minute—you can't run around naked—put these on.

Through the open window we hear a band strike up

Oh, that's all we need—a bloody band—put these on and run.

The band goes into a rousing French march, all drums and trumpets. Stanley hauls the loose rope through the window and hurls it under Bed Two and then, completely and utterly exhausted, he throws himself on to Bed One among the tangled bedding and lies there on his back in his underwear. The band now goes off in the distance. Stanley lies on the bed panting for a moment or two and then the door opens

Claude enters, looks at Stanley, the disordered bedclothes, and draws his own conclusions

Claude You dirty, filthy beast! What the hell have you been doing?
Stanley (*panting*) Nothing.
Claude Nothing? You're an animal, that's what you are. An animal!

Claude goes to the bathroom door and, opening it, looks in

All right. Where is she?
Stanley She's gone.
Claude Gone where?
Stanley (*panting*) She went while you were downstairs.
Claude She would have passed me on the way down. (*He crosses and looks under Bed Two*)
Stanley What are you doing?
Claude Well she's here somewhere—dead or alive. (*He pulls out the coil of rope, looks at it, and then looks at Stanley in growing horror*) What have you been doing with that woman and this rope? Are you some sort of sexual deviate?
Stanley Oh, it's not mine. It was left there by the previous tenant.
Claude They would have found it when they swept under the beds.
Stanley (*gasping*) What makes you think they sweep under the beds?
Claude Well, perhaps you're right. (*He goes to the wardrobe*) Well she's in here somewhere.

Claude slides open the wardrobe door revealing Stanley's suitcase and coat. Stanley gets off the bed

Stanley (*shouting*) Wait! (*He advances on Claude with a Quasimodo-type walk*)
Claude (*turning*) Yes? (*He cowers back at Stanley's approach*)

Stanley lunges at the wardrobe and grabs his car coat then he points to the wallpapered door

Stanley She's through there.
Claude Through where?
Stanley Through the wallpaper.

Claude goes to the wallpapered door to examine it. Stanley pulls his case out, puts it on Bed One, opens it and pulls out another pair of slacks and a pullover. He dresses rapidly over the following conversation

Claude You mean that's the room next door?
Stanley Yes, she lives in there.
Claude Well why the hell didn't you say so before?

Stanley Why should I tell you about my personal friends?

But Claude has seen the radiator. He looks at it in disbelief and points

Claude The radiator.
Stanley (*casually*) What about it?
Claude What's it doing up there?
Stanley I've no idea.
Claude It wasn't there before.
Stanley Yes it was.
Claude No, it wasn't . . .
Stanley Yes, it was . . . Oh look, if we're going to share the room, we might as well try and get along together. (*As he says this he rearranges the contents of his suitcase. In doing so he lifts out a bottle of cognac*)
Claude (*eyeing the bottle*) Well, if you're offering me a drink . . .
Stanley Yes, of course I am.
Claude Well come along, then. Open it up.
Stanley Eh? Oh not *this*, I'm taking this back to England with me. I'll buy you one.
Claude Good. I'll order some.
Stanley Thank you very much.

Claude goes over to the telephone. Stanley, meanwhile, puts his cognac back in his case and repacks it

Claude (*on the phone*) Hello? . . . Can we have some drinks, please? . . . Yes, I know the bar's closed. I mean up here. . . . Good. I'll have a double Scotch.
Stanley I'll have three.
Claude (*on the phone*) You'd better send the whole bottle up. Thank you. (*He hangs up and starts moving to the wardrobe*) Now look, old boy. I know we're in France, but while I'm here, no more ropes or radiators. Please.

Before Stanley can stop him, he slams one wardrobe door shut in order to open the other one

Stanley No—wait—that's my end.
Claude Your end?
Stanley Yes. This is your end—God willing.

Stanley pulls the other door and it slides back with no trouble. Inside is his car coat. He takes it out

There we are. All clear.
Claude But my suit is at your end.
Stanley Ah—I'll get it. (*He gets into the wardrobe*) It's easier this way, I promise you.
Claude Easier?
Stanley Oh much easier. Yes.

Stanley slams the door in Claude's face. Claude sighs and waits

Claude What are you doing in there?

Stanley (*inside the wardrobe*) Shan't be a second.

Claude loses patience. He pulls open the door and reveals Stanley with Helga's clothing all bundled up in his arms. Claude does not recognize them

Stanley I was just hanging my wife's clothing up from the inside—up the other end.

Stanley edges down the wardrobe and vanishes. Claude reaches in and takes out his suit and then he closes the door. He goes to open the other door but this time it has stuck. He tugs at it for a while, then he tries to open the first door again, but that also has stuck

Claude I say—you in there.

Stanley (*inside the wardrobe*) Yes?

Claude The doors have jammed.

Stanley (*inside the wardrobe*) Well get 'em open—I'll suffocate!

Claude Serves you right. You shouldn't have gone in there.

Claude makes a half-hearted attempt to open the doors

The main door of the room opens and Karak enters with a bottle and glasses on a tray. He hands the tray to Claude

Karak Eh, voilà—and is finish of room service.

Karak runs to the window and opens it

Claude Here, what are you doing? Close that window.

Karak We are all watching her from downstairs.

Claude Watching who?

Karak Is naked woman running around in woods.

Claude Naked woman?

Claude joins Karak at the window. The wardrobe door opens and Stanley looks out. Seeing that Claude and Karak are occupied looking out of the window, Stanley seizes his chance and holding Helga's clothing and her suitcase he runs to the main door

Stanley exits

Karak Well is festival time. You are seeing her?

Claude No.

Karak She was creeping towards hotel, and then she see me looking. She turn and run off into woods.

Claude Well, if you ask me, it's damn disgraceful.

They turn away from the window

Good job my wife isn't here.

Karak (*puzzled*) Your wife is not here?

Claude No, of course she isn't.

Karak Ah, you are right. Lady I am showing up here is belonging to other man.

Claude Well it must be his wife. His girlfriend's in there. (*He points to the wallpapered door*)

Karak But Mrs Hoffmeyer is in that room.

Claude Oh, that's her name, is it? What's she like?

Karak I am not seeing her, but she is Bulgarian lady, who is doing things with bicycles.

Claude Doing things with bicycles?

Karak Ja, der manager is hoping she brings good business to hotel.

Claude (*picking up the rope*) I think she's already started.

Karak So where is other man's *wife*?

Claude I've no idea. (*He turns to the wardrobe*) Good heavens, he's gone.

Simone enters. Slim and attractive. She is a cabaret dancer. Tough and very worldly, she has, however, a wild and outrageous sense of humour. She speaks with a slight French accent. She carries a suitcase

Simone Hello, darling.

Claude Simone!

Claude and Simone embrace

I didn't think you could make it.

Simone I will explain in a moment, darling. Where's the bathroom?

Claude It's through there.

Simone What a lovely big room—with two beds—ooh! Naughty boy.

Simone puts her case down and exits to the bathroom

Claude turns to face Karak who is giving him a curious look

Karak So, who is that lady?

Claude (*taking out his wallet*) Don't be so ridiculous, my dear fellow. That lady is my wife.

He hands Karak a ten-franc note. Karak looks at it

Karak Not for ten francs she's not.

Claude starts to hand him more money, as—

the CURTAIN *falls*

ACT II

The same. Five minutes later

Simone is sitting on Bed Two holding a compact. Claude is standing above her

Claude You look absolutely gorgeous, my dear.
Simone Thank you. I hope he approves of me.
Claude Who?
Simone This man we are sharing the room with.
Claude Oh him—don't worry about him. We'll soon get rid of him. You see I didn't know you were coming.

Simone crosses and hangs her coat in the wardrobe

Simone I told you. This job came up. A cabaret. I couldn't turn it down.
Claude No, of course not. But I booked this damned great room and when I arrived there was a message from you saying you couldn't make it.

Claude pours her a drink and hands it to her

Simone Well, I finished my act by eight-thirty so I drove straight here. (*She looks at the whisky bottle*) Oh, darling. You know I only drink cognac.
Claude There's a bottle in his case if he hasn't locked it.

Claude goes to the wardrobe, opens Stanley's case and pulls out a bottle of cognac

Simone Who?
Claude That idiot they've put in with us.
Simone But where is he?
Claude He's gone to look at some naked woman running around in the woods.
Simone But what kind of an hotel is this?
Claude The only one with a vacancy.
Simone That doesn't surprise me.

They raise their glasses

Claude To us, my dear.
Simone To us, darling.

They sit on Bed Two and drink. A short pause

How is your wife?
Claude Oh, she's quite well, thank you.

Simone Is she still cold towards you?

Claude Yes. Yes, she is. (*He sighs*) In fact at this moment she's colder than ever.

Simone Why don't you divorce her?

Claude No, darling, we've been through all that. I can't.

Simone But you don't love her.

Claude Well, yes and no. You see she's an excellent wife. Awfully clean.

Simone Clean?

Claude Awfully clean, yes. The house is spotless, the furniture spotless. Even the garden's spotless.

Simone (*without interest*) Oh, really.

Claude Yes—I'm not sure but sometimes I think she even Hoovers the flower beds. (*He sighs*) You've no idea how clean she is. In fact she's so clean that when it's time for bed, she looks at me with those clean blue eyes and I feel absolutely filthy. And I go right off.

Simone Yes, you go off to cabarets and pick up girls like me, yes?

Claude Now that's not fair.

Simone It's true though, isn't it?

Claude No, no, no. I didn't pick you up—I *met* you—I only went in there on business.

Simone (*mocking him*) Business?

Claude (*rising*) Yes, business. You *know* what my business is. (*He sits on Bed One, facing her*)

Simone Ah, so you came in the night club to sell us *biscuits*?

Claude No, not *you*. The chap I was with. He's one of our best customers. He dragged me in there.

Simone And I dragged you out.

Claude Did you really? I can't really remember . . . I'd had a few.

Simone Oh, you had. You gave me a tin of custard creams.

Claude Oh, so that's what happened to them.

Simone (*rising*) I am going for a bath.

She suddenly reacts at the sight of the radiator. She points to it and Claude looks round at it

What the hell is *that*?

Claude Yes, I know. He did it.

Simone But *how*?

Claude I can't imagine. You see he had a woman up here. They did it between them.

Simone (*intrigued*) Well, I've heard óf some curious things, but with *radiators*?

Simone begins to unpack her case, she takes from it a dressing-gown

Claude I think he's a bit kinky. Or she is—or perhaps they both are.

Simone Where is she?

Claude She's in the room next door and her name is Mrs Hoffmeyer.

Simone Well, why doesn't he go in there with her? (*She takes a nun's gown from her suitcase*)

Claude I don't know. Darling. Perhaps he *is* in there.

Simone Well let's hope he stays in there. I don't want him in here with us.

Claude (*intrigued*) I say . . . is that a nun's outfit?

Simone Yes.

Claude Do you wear that in your cabaret?

Simone Yes. But not for long—I wear *this* underneath. (*She takes out a black corset with red bows and holds it to her waist*)

Claude Are you—er—putting it on?

Simone My act?

Claude No, no. The underwear.

Simone But I've just taken it off.

Claude Pity.

Simone (*sexily*) You want me to put it on again for you? Yes?

Claude Well—er—only if you want to.

Simone And then take it off again, *oui*?

Claude Well—er—only if you want to.

Simone (*sitting on his knee*) You want a private performance?

Claude Well, why not? I haven't seen your new cabaret have I?

Simone Well, it comes rather expensive . . .

Claude (*archly*) Ahhh yes, but you wait until you see what you're getting for it.

She looks at him, tongue in cheek

Simone Would you mind if I saw it first?

Claude Well, er . . .

Simone Oh, can't you show it to me now?

Claude I was hoping to save it for later. Still.

Claude brings out a jewel case. He gives it to Simone, who looks surprised

Simone Oh, is this it? (*She sits on Bed One*)

Claude Why, what were you expecting?

Simone I didn't know—I thought it might be another tin of biscuits. (*She opens the case and takes out a diamond bracelet. She is obviously delighted with it*) Oh, darling, it's lovely. It must have cost a fortune.

Claude (*modestly*) Yes, it was rather expensive.

Simone (*pushing him back and kissing him*) Oh, I'm sure it was. Thank you, darling. (*Leaping up*) It's cabaret time.

Simone goes back to her suitcase. She puts down the bracelet and picks up her transistor radio. She switches it on. There is a Tyrolean band playing. Although the music is somewhat inappropriate for a strip-tease number she starts to remove her dress in sexy stripper style, during which she puts her hat on Claude's head, and her dress round his shoulders. Under her dress she is wearing a slip which she keeps on. Claude watches her, giving long growls of approval. She strikes a pose

Claude Is that the end of it?

Simone For the moment, yes. Second performance—at midnight.

Simone picks up the radio set, the nun's outfit, the dressing-gown, and the bracelet. Still with her sexy dancing movement, she moves to the bathroom door and exits

Claude gives a long growl of lust and then there is a knocking at the main door

Heinz (*off*) It's the Manager.
Claude Clear out.
Heinz (*off*) Your wife is here.
Claude (*screaming*) Clear ou—— My wife!!?

Simone runs out of the bathroom

Simone Your wife? You *imbecile.*

Simone runs back into the bathroom

Claude, in a frenzy, rises off the bed and starts throwing all evidence of Simone into her case. He fastens one catch and puts the case by Bed Two. He has, however, forgotten he is still wearing her hat

Heinz (*off*) Would you unlock this door, please?
Claude Yes, yes, yes. I'm coming. I'm coming. (*He straightens his tie and, with a final look round the room, runs to the main door and opens it*)
Heinz This way, dear lady.

A cowled figure in monk's garb enters. It is not immediately recognizable as Helga. Heinz, still in his feathers, follows her in

Claude, looking for his wife, looks outside in the hall. Puzzled, he shuts the door. Helga sits down on the pouffe, facing front

Claude What the hell . . . Oh, sorry, Father. (*He takes his hat off in deference to the monk*) I thought you said my wife . . .

Helga turns towards him and raises her head

Helga Hello, Claude.
Claude (*incredulously*) *Helga!* What the hell goes on? And why are you dressed like——
Heinz (*cutting in*) Your wife has had an unfortunate experience.
Claude You mean she's become a *monk*? No, she can't have. She's a Protestant—anyway, my wife's married. Helga, you haven't, have you?
Helga Oh, don't be ridiculous, Claude. What happened was . . . (*She feels a sneeze coming on. She puckers her face awaiting it, it is a long time coming*) Handkerchief, somebody.

Heinz, ever the gentleman, whips a lace handkerchief from his sleeve and hands it to her. She sneezes. Claude, suddenly aware of Simone's hat, whips it behind his back and, as Helga sneezes, he throws it into the open wardrobe

Heinz I gather she was soaked through.
Claude But what happened to her?

Helga goes to speak and then feels another sneeze coming on

Heinz She tells me she was in the village pond.
Claude I thought she was in Heidelberg.
Heinz No, no, no. Apparently she drove her car into the pond and all her clothes were soaking wet.
Claude Helga, you're not hurt, are you?
Helga No, I'm not hurt. But I had to take off all my wet—(*another sneeze is coming on*)—clothes. (*The sneeze prevents further speech*)
Heinz Fortunately, she found Saint Wolfgang.
Claude And borrowed his?
Heinz Exactly.
Claude (*puzzled*) Well what's *he* wearing?
Heinz Oh, nothing at the moment.
Claude I see.
Heinz Oh, not the *real* Saint Wolfgang. The dummy. The one we are burning.
Claude Oh, I see.
Heinz Yes, it's in a cart at the back of the hotel. You know the legend, of course?

Helga is once more about to sneeze

Claude (*vaguely*) Legend?
Heinz (*giving it the full drama*) Yes. He was to be burned at the stake, but the village people believed him innocent, so at the last moment they substituted a dummy—which was burned in his place. He was accused of witchcraft and adultery.
Claude (*shooting a guilty look at the bathroom*) Ad . . . ad . . . Adultery?
Heinz Adultery.
Claude Oh—adultery. Serves him right. Er—by the way, did you—er— tell my wife you'd let the room to somebody else?
Heinz I mentioned it. Yes.
Helga Yes, he said there was another man in here with you.
Claude (*glancing at the bathroom*) Yes. Oh, there is, yes, and a nasty piece of work, too. You see I didn't know you were coming.
Helga No. Well, as it was your birthday, I thought I would surprise you.
Claude And you did—you certainly did. Yes.
Helga Many happy returns.
Claude Thank you. Yes. And now we'll have to find a room somewhere else, won't we?
Helga Somewhere else? But you have a roo—— (*she sneezes*)
Claude Oh, we can't stay here. No, we'll leave. Yes, we'll both leave, right away. (*He lifts Helga to her feet*) This very moment.

Helga Oh no—I've caught cold. I must have a hot bath.

Claude shoots a guilty look at the bathroom and sits Helga back on the pouffe

Claude Impossible. Out of the question.
Heinz Why is it? (*He lifts Helga up. To Helga*) Of *course* you may have a hot bath.
Claude (*sitting Helga down again*) No she can't. Not in there.
Heinz Why not?
Helga Yes, why not?
Claude Because this other man's wife is in there. (*He backs towards the bathroom*)
Helga Your room-mate's wife?
Claude Yes, she's in there—bathing away—so you see the sooner we leave the better.
Heinz You mean she has come back?
Claude Obviously.
Heinz (*moving to the bathroom*) I would like to see her.

Claude runs to the bathroom and puts his hand over the keyhole

Claude Oh no you don't.
Heinz I mean when she comes out.
Claude Oh, when she comes out. We'll *all* see her, won't we?
Heinz Of course.
Claude Only she may not be out for quite a time.
Heinz Why?
Claude She's had a long trip and she's soaking.

Helga sneezes

Heinz So is your wife. Perhaps we can ask her to hurry up?
Claude Oh, we can't do that. Surely that's up to her husband.

The main door opens and Stanley enters. He looks confused and weary. He closes the door and leans against it

Oh, there you are. We've been looking for you.
Stanley Have you?
Heinz Your wife is here.

Helga, self-possessed, turns and looks at him coolly

Helga Hello.
Stanley That's not my wife.
Claude No, that's *my* wife, you idiot.
Helga How do you do?
Stanley (*uneasily*) Oh. How do you do?
Heinz She has returned.
Stanley So I see, yes. I—er—didn't recognize her.

Helga (*coldly*) No, there is no reason why you should. We have never met before.

Stanley (*confused*) No—no, of course not, no—I thought she was a monk, and I thought, well, he wouldn't be married to a monk, would he?

Helga No.

Stanley No—a nun possibly—no . . . He wouldn't be married to a nun either, would he?

Helga No.

Stanley No, I didn't recognize her as a *woman*, that's what I mean.

Claude Have you finished?

Stanley Yes, and I'm leaving. (*He starts to go*)

Heinz Your wife has returned and she is in the bathroom.

Stanley (*surprised*) Oh, Brenda?

Claude If that is her name.

Stanley Did she find her ring?

Stanley goes to the bathroom, and Claude goes with him. Stanley knocks on the door

(*Shouting*) Brenda!

Claude (*shouting*) Your husband's here, Brenda—and my wife has arrived —er—Brenda.

Stanley looks at him suspiciously

Stanley Why are you calling my wife Brenda?

Claude Because that's her name—I mean there's no point in standing on ceremony if we're to share the room.

Stanley What, the four of us?

Claude Er, no. No, we're leaving, right away.

Helga Oh no, not until I've had a bath.

Stanley I'll tell her to hurry up. (*Banging on the door*) Hurry up, Brenda.

Claude (*hastily*) It's all right, darling . . .

Stanley *Darling?*

Claude Did I say darling?

Helga is not listening, she is sneezing. Heinz is more concerned with Helga

Heinz I think your wife should have a hot bath immediately. That is my medical opinion.

Claude Well, nobody asked you for it.

Heinz Nevertheless. She should have a bath.

Claude (*impatiently*) Very well then, give her one.

Heinz (*pleasantly surprised*) You want me to *bath* her?

Claude No, no. I mean *find* her a bath. There must be other bathrooms in this rat-trap.

Heinz I'm afraid they are all occupied.

Claude What about you?

Heinz Me?

Claude Surely *you* have a bath?

Heinz (*with hurt pride*) Of course I have a bath. I have a bath every day, sometimes even two.

Claude Well, what do you bath in?

Heinz Hot water, naturally.

Claude (*in despair*) Oh for heaven's sake.

Heinz (*irritatedly*) Well, what do you expect me to bath in? Asses' milk? Champagne? Really, you know, I don't have to stand this abuse from you. I am the Manager.

Claude Then do you think you could manage to let my wife borrow your bathroom?

Heinz Of course. Why didn't you ask me in the first place. Anyone would think I was some kind of an idiot. This way, dear lady.

Helga sneezes. Heinz turns to lead her to the door and suddenly stops in horror as he sees the radiator

Lieber Gott, have we had an explosion?

Helga I merely sneezed.

Heinz No, no. The radiator! What's it doing up there?

They all look at the radiator

Claude Ask the Marquis De Sade.

They all look at Stanley

Stanley (*flustered*) That's been playing up all day, that has. It's been leaking and banging—and leaking—I think it's on its last legs.

Heinz (*icily*) It's on the *ceiling.*

Stanley Yes—yes—well that's steam pressure.

Heinz Steam pressure?

Stanley Yes, steam pressure. The pressure of steam—it presses, and expands and the power's—enormous . . .

Heinz It couldn't do that. That's impossible.

Stanley (*wildly*) Why not? I mean steam pressure can drive locomotives, and ocean liners, and battleships, and—why shouldn't it drive a radiator?

Claude *I* have never heard such rubbish.

Stanley Then don't listen to it.

Helga Could I have my bath please?

Heinz (*looking at the radiator*) Yes, of course, dear lady. (*He leads her to the main door*)

Helga (*firmly*) I'm afraid I'm not only wet, I'm in great discomfort. It's like wearing sand-paper.

Heinz Well monks wear them all the time, you know.

Heinz and Helga exit

Stanley You're taking a bit of a chance, aren't you?

Claude (*with feeling*) Oh, I have been, yes. (*Realizing*) Eh? What do you mean?

Stanley Letting her go off with him.

Claude (*alarmed*) Well he wouldn't try anything . . . Would he?
Stanley He did with my wife.
Claude Well you might have warned me.

Claude runs to the door and then hesitates, torn between two conflicting emotions

Stanley (*knocking on the bathroom door*) Brenda.

This decides Claude, who returns quickly

Claude No, no, my wife is quite capable of taking care of herself. I won't bother. Not to worry.
Stanley She'll need to with him.
Claude My wife is absolutely and completely respectable.
Stanley So was mine—until she came here.
Claude (*coldly*) I wouldn't know that. I've never met your wife.
Stanley Never met her? You keep calling her darling.
Claude Ah yes. Well, I think perhaps I'd better explain. You see—(*he points to the bathroom*)—the lady in the bathroom is not your Brenda.
Stanley (*baffled*) Well, who is she?
Claude A friend.
Stanley A friend of Brenda's?
Claude A friend of *mine*.

Stanley is finally enlightened

Stanley Oh, I see. Now I *see*.
Claude No, you don't see, you don't see it at all. It's all absolutely innocent.
Stanley You've got a bird in there.
Claude (*coldly*) I have a *lady* in there. There's no need to be coarse or vulgar about it.
Stanley (*sarcastically*) Oh no. Oh no, no—let's not be coarse or vulgar, oh no, when I had a lady up here you accused me of bringing some cheap tart up here . . .
Claude Well, I was wrong—very, very wrong, and I apologize. I am sure Mrs Hoffmeyer is a perfect lady.

Claude sits on the armchair and pours a drink

Stanley (*puzzled*) Who?
Claude Mrs Hoffmeyer. The Bulgarian lady with the bicycle tricks, your friend from next door.

Claude gives Stanley a puzzled look as he points to the wallpapered door

Stanley Oh her. Yes, I—er—only knew her by her first name.
Claude (*kindly*) And what's that?
Stanley (*hesitantly*) Gladys.
Claude (*surprised*) Gladys Hoffmeyer?
Stanley (*hastily*) Yes. What about yours in the bathroom?
Claude Oh, her name is Simone.

Stanley (*mocking him*) Oh, Simone, I might have known.
Claude Now look, old chap—I need your help.

Claude adopts a friendly and beseeching tone towards Stanley. Stanley moves to Bed Two, sits on the end of it and flicks open a magazine

Stanley Oh yes, you need my help—and a fat lot of help you gave me when *I* needed it. What was it you called me?
Claude Let's not dwell in the past. (*He moves over to Stanley*) You see, any of us is liable to be the victim of a situation which puts us in a bad light.
Stanley You're not in a bad light, mate, you're floodlit. You are fully illuminated and it's showing you up for the mealy mouthed hypocrite you are. You want me to pretend that woman in there is my wife.

Claude glares at him balefully

Claude Well, it won't be for long. As soon as Helga is ready we shall leave.
Stanley And I shall be alone with *Simone*.
Claude Oh no, you won't, because she'll be leaving as well.
Stanley Oh, will she?
Claude (*persuasively*) Yes—you'll have the entire room to yourself. You can do exactly what you like up here—you and Gladys—the ropes, the radiators and the bicycles. It'll be like Chipperfield's circus.
Stanley (*shaking his head*) No.
Claude (*sitting by Stanley*) Now listen, old chap, what *is* your name by the way?
Stanley Stanley.
Claude (*sonorously*) Stanley. What a manly name, Stanley. I'm Claude. (*He extends a hand, which Stanley ignores*)
Stanley So will I be, if Brenda comes back.
Claude (*with faint menace*) Then let's trust she never hears about Gladys Hoffmeyer.
Stanley (*warily*) Well she won't, will she? I mean, how will she?
Claude Well you know how people gossip, especially one's enemies.
Stanley I haven't got any enemies.

Claude laughs unpleasantly and rises

The door opens and Heinz enters

Heinz Your wife needs some clothing.
Claude Clothing?
Heinz Yes. A dress, underwear. The usual things ladies wear, when they're not dressed as monks.
Claude Well, I haven't got anything. Where are her clothes?
Heinz She said perhaps this gentleman might help.

They both look at Stanley, who puts a hand to his brow as if trying to remember something

Stanley I think—I thought I saw a lady's coat and a suitcase by the back door.

Claude (*without suspicion*) Thank you. I'll go and see if it's hers.

Heinz Would you please? Only we are needing the monk's robe for Saint Wolfgang.

Heinz exits

Claude moves to the door and turns

Claude Oh, and about that other business with Brenda and Gladys. I trust you'll be sensible.

Claude exits

Stanley gives a loud, deep sigh and goes to the armchair. He gives another sigh and pours himself a drink of cognac. He sighs again and sips the cognac, worn out by all his efforts

Simone comes out of the bathroom quietly and crosses slowly to the armchair

She looks down at Stanley, her leg close to the armchair. She wears her dressing-gown tied loosely over her black stage underwear. Stanley, who has been facing away from her, slowly turns and does a take. Then turns away and pours himself another drink rapidly, giving an extra loud sigh. Then he slowly examines her from legs to face. She smiles at him. And he gives her a sickly grin in return. His glass is almost overflowing

Stanley (*rising and backing away*) I was—just having a sip of your cognac.

Simone (*casually*) Help yourself, pour me one. (*She sits on the arm of the chair and sizes him up*)

Stanley pours her a drink and lifts his own up

Stanley Oh—I've got rather a big one. It's rather nice, isn't it? I've got a bottle like this. I'm taking it back to England, you know, duty free.

Simone Are you?

Stanley Yes, cheers.

Simone Cheers.

Stanley Yes, I saw this here and I knew it wasn't his, so I presume it's yours?

Simone (*directly*) No, it's yours.

Stanley (*astounded*) Mine. You mean you took that out of my case?

Simone I didn't, Claude did. He said you wouldn't mind.

Stanley (*angrily*) Why, the rotten, thieving swine.

Simone But obviously you do.

Stanley I'll kill him.

Simone (*dispassionately*) Good, I'll help you bury him.
Stanley (*angrily*) I was taking that back to England with me. He thinks
   he can get away with anything. (*He sits on the pouffe*)
Simone I agree.
Stanley It's typical of that sort of Englishman. Just because he's in the
   Diplomatic Corps.
Simone In the *what*?
Stanley The Diplomatic Corps.
Simone Ooh. He sells biscuits.
Stanley *Biscuits?* Oh, you can't believe anything he says, can you? He's
   a liar—and a thief—(*looking at the cognac*)—and a . . .
Simone Miser.
Stanley I'll bet he is.

*Simone, who up to now has been rather cool, starts to grow annoyed at the
thought of Claude's misdeeds*

Simone Do you know, he just gave me a diamond bracelet. I took it in
   the bathroom to see if it would cut glass . . .
Stanley And did it?
Simone The diamonds fell out, only they weren't diamonds.
Stanley Oh that's typical of him, typical.
Simone (*angrily*) You know what he usually gives me?
Stanley What?
Simone Tins of biscuits.
Stanley What?
Simone Tins of biscuits, and they're usually broken, and you know what
   he expects in return?
Stanley Well . . .
Simone (*angrily*) Oh, he expects a girl to be madly in love with him, to
   flatter him, to run around after him, and to—and to . . . You know, to
   make love to him and to do all these things—and for what? I mean, if
   you were a girl, would *you* do it?
Stanley Well, not for broken biscuits.
Simone Also he is so madly jealous of me, I can't look at another man.
   Well, I promise you, I'll make him so jealous he'll—explode. (*She kneels
   by Stanley*)
Stanley Good idea, love, you find yourself another feller.
Simone (*cold-bloodedly*) Don't worry, I've found one.
Stanley Good. Who?
Simone You. (*She puts her hand on his leg*)
Stanley (*rising in alarm*) Me?
Simone Oui.

*She jerks him forward so that he is kneeling on the pouffe. He puts his hands
on her bottom to steady himself—and then lets go*

Stanley No. (*He rises*)
Simone Yes. Look, he wants you to pretend we are married, yes?
Stanley (*alarmed*) *No!* (*He takes a step back from the pouffe*)

Simone (*ignoring him*) So we shall pretend. We'll pretend so hard he'll break a blood vessel *watching us.*

She lies back across the pouffe, her head towards Stanley, who looks down at her in fascinated horror

Stanley Watching us? When you say watching us . . . Watching us what?
Simone Oh, come on, darling—you are a man of the world.
Stanley No—I've never been abroad before.
Simone (*rising*) Well don't worry, baby . . . I'll take you on a guided tour.

Stanley retreats from her

Stanley I'd rather you didn't—you see my wife . . .
Simone (*following him*) Won't find out.
Stanley She might.
Simone (*tiger-like*) She won't if I don't tell her.
Stanley (*aghast*) *Tell* her?
Simone About you and Mrs Hoffmeyer. But I won't tell her providing you . . .

Simone caresses Stanley, running her hands over him. She pulls up his trouser leg and feels his leg

Stanley Providing I co-operate?
Simone Co-operate. Yes, we shall co-operate for Claude's sake. (*She pushes him down so that he sits on the foot of Bed Two*)
Stanley But Claude is leaving, isn't he?
Simone You think he will go and leave me here with you? Not if I know him.
Stanley (*timidly*) Can I ask something? How far are we going?
Simone We are going to bed.

He looks at the bed and realizes the implications

Stanley (*with mixed emotions*) Are we? Well—if I'm being blackmailed into it . . .
Simone (*kneeling on the bed above him*) Oh, that's an ugly word.
Stanley Well, I mean, coerced. You know—persuaded by threats.
Simone Oh, couldn't you just think of it as fun, baby? (*She fingers his knee*)
Stanley Oh no. I couldn't think of it as fun.
Simone (*suddenly sexy*) And why not, darling?
Stanley Well you see, my conscience would make me feel very guilty.
Simone (*with mock concern*) Would it, baby? (*She lies across his lap*)
Stanley Oh yes, if I thought of it as fun. But if I thought of it as a necessary duty to save my marriage as a task to be fulfilled—as it were.
Simone Well, try and look as if you are enjoying it for Claude's sake.
Stanley But Claude won't be there, will he? Not when we . . .
Simone Oh, it's for his *benefit.* (*She sits up*)
Stanley (*very firmly*) Oh, I'm sorry. I don't give benefit performances.

Simone ignores his last remark, as she stands and picks up her case

Simone (*intensely*) You wait. Tonight I shall give the greatest show he has
  ever seen. (*She starts to gyrate slowly as she speaks in anticipation of her
  act*)
Stanley Will you?
Simone I shall be magnificent, the greatest performance of my career.
Stanley What actually *is* your career?
Simone You'll find out, darling, you're going to be in the audience.
Stanley *Audience?*
Simone Don't go away, my darling husband.

They kiss lightly

I'm going to get dressed.

Simone gyrates her way to the bathroom and exits

Stanley Get dressed? Hardly seems worth while, does it? (*He suddenly
  runs and leaps over the pouffe in delight. He growls, gives the pouffe a
  kick, and goes to the armchair. He sits on it and rubs his thighs. He
  chuckles*)

The main door opens and Claude enters

Claude Now we're in trouble. Helga refuses to go, insists upon staying the
  night here.
Stanley (*indicating the bathroom*) Yes, and I've been alone with Simone—
  and so does she.
Claude Oh, does she?
Stanley Yes. You ask her.
Claude Well that's all right, I've spoken to the Manager and he's putting
  a camp-bed in the bathroom.
Stanley Who for?
Claude You.
Stanley Why me? (*He rises*)
Claude Isn't that obvious?
Stanley (*growing angry*) Not to me it isn't. I started off here with a large
  room with two double beds in it. Then I have a room with one double
  bed in it. Now I've got a camp-bed in the bathroom. Before this is over
  I'll be on the roof in a bloody hammock.
Claude Don't be so awkward. (*He picks up the bottle from the table*)
Stanley (*babbling*) Awkward? I'm fighting for my very existence—here,
  what with you—and her—and the other one—and—lying and hiding
  and, and—pretending—and you've opened my brandy. I'm supposed to
  be on *holiday*.

He grapples with Claude for the bottle

Claude (*severely*) All right, don't get so hysterical. I know it's a difficult
  situation, but if we both pull together, we shall both get out of it.

Stanley But I don't have to get out of it. I'm not in it, you're the one who's in it, mate.

Stanley ends up with the bottle and puts it on the table

Claude Aren't you forgetting Gladys Hoffmeyer?

Stanley Oh, to hell with Gladys Hoffmeyer. (*He gets his case from the wardrobe*)

Claude (*moving to Stanley*) It's a little late for that, Stanley my boy, we are in this together. United we stand, divided we fall, and you are sleeping in the bathroom. (*He grabs Stanley's case and moves away from him*)

Stanley (*bitterly*) And where are you sleeping? Or do you intend making a tour?

Claude That is no concern of yours.

Stanley grabs his case from Claude

Stanley Well it should be, I am supposed to be married to her.

Claude Very well then, you sleep in separate beds. There's nothing unusual in that. Helga and I do.

Stanley Well, Simone and I don't. You ask her.

Claude Simone?

Stanley Yes.

Claude (*horrified*) You don't think she wants you in bed with her, do you?

Helga enters, now dressed and carrying her coat, suitcase, and the monk's robe

Helga Who?

Claude Who what, dear?

Helga (*She puts all her gear on Bed Two*) Who doesn't want who, in bed with who?

Claude (*indicating Stanley*) Ah, his wife, Brenda, doesn't want him in bed with her.

Helga Oh, why?

Claude Well, that's no concern of ours—darling.

Helga Well, you seem to be discussing it—I mean, why?

Claude Why? Well—er—he has a rash.

Helga A rash?

Claude Yes, he was showing it to me. It's on his . . . I don't like the look of it.

Helga (*to Stanley*) Is it bad?

Stanley I don't know. Ask *him*.

Helga Well, Claude wouldn't know. Would you mind if I saw it?

Claude Of course he would. Darling, you can't go around examining people's rashes.

Helga You seem to forget I was two years in a skin hospital and three years in a fever hospital and five years in—that hospital where I met you.

Stanley (*whispering, interested*) What was wrong with *him*?
Claude I had a little trouble with my . . . You mind your own business.
Stanley It's as much my business, as my rash is your business.
Helga Ah, but his was not infectious. And yours might be.
Stanley No it's not.
Helga How do you know? After all, we are sharing the room . . .
Claude Oh no, we're not. He's sleeping in the bathroom.
Helga All the same I think I should see it. Now where is it?
Claude It's near his . . . stomach.
Stanley What?!
Helga Then let me see it.

Helga advances on Stanley, the full no-nonsense nursing sister

Stanley It's not very handy, actually. (*He retreats towards the bathroom door*)
Helga Oh, come on. Let me look at it.
Stanley No. It's on the move.
Helga (*sternly*) Just lift up your shirt and let me look at it.

The bathroom door opens and Simone emerges, wearing her dress. She reacts in mock horror

Simone Look at what, madame?
Helga (*now embarrassed*) I was just asking your husband to let me see his . . .
Simone (*pretending shock*) Well *really*, madame! Do you think he is showing it to everyone?
Claude Now, now, ladies. My wife meant well, after all, it was her profession.
Simone Well, you know her profession better than I do, monsieur.
Stanley (*defending Helga*) No, it's true. I mean—she was a nurse.
Simone Oh, was she, darling. (*Putting an arm around Stanley's neck*) Well, if there's anything wrong with you, I think as your wife, I should be the one to see it. (*And grabbing Stanley by the arm she yanks him into the bathroom*)
Stanley Back in a second.

Simone and Stanley exit

Helga Well—poor man.
Claude Poor man? What do you mean, poor man?
Helga Well, married to a woman like her, and he seems so nice.
Claude (*snorting*) Nice? He's not nice, he's revolting.
Helga Oh, how do you know?
Claude Because I've been up here with him, he's a complete degenerate . . .

The bathroom door opens and Simone emerges, followed by a very embarrassed-looking Stanley

Helga Did you see it, madame?
Simone I did, and I assure you, it's nothing to worry about.
Helga Well, was it inflamed?
Simone (*after thinking for a moment*) I don't know what you mean.
Helga I mean was it angry looking?
Simone Er, no. It seemed quite peaceful to me.
Helga Oh, good.
Simone (*to Stanley*) Are you ready, darling?
Stanley (*alarmed*) Ready for what?
Simone To go out for a drink?
Stanley (*with feeling*) Oh—that's something I am ready for.

Simone goes to the door, followed by Stanley. As they reach it, it flies open, nearly knocking Stanley over

Karak enters, carrying a camp-bed

Karak Where you are wantink bed?
Stanley Oh, we don't need it now, thank you . . .

Stanley exits with Simone

Karak looks baffled

Claude Oh yes we do. Put it in the bathroom.
Karak But man with your wife said . . .
Claude This lady is *my* wife, that lady is *his* wife.

Karak looks at them both. They both look guilty

Karak (*impassively*) Of course, monsieur, I am makink mistake. (*He puts the bed by the bathroom door*)
Helga Here is your robe. (*She looks around for the monk's robe and picks it up*)
Karak Robe?
Helga Yes, the monk's habit. The Manager said you would be needing it for the festival.
Karak Manager is idiot. (*He takes the robe to the window, opens the window, and throws it out*) Is not tyink *me* up to bonfire. One nasty accident mit matches and ohoh—Saint Wolfgank, he is goink off with a poof.
Claude How very unpleasant.
Karak (*in surprise*) Hey—what is happening to radiator?
Claude I shudder to think.
Karak Does madame know?
Claude How would she know, she wasn't here.
Karak What are you sayink? She wasn't here?
Helga (*coldly*) He means *I* wasn't here.
Karak But I am showink you up here to room, we are talkink . . .
Claude (*puzzled*) Talking?

Helga On the stairs. You see I got lost on my way down from the Manager's bathroom. (*She hangs her coat in the wardrobe*)

Claude Well if you got lost on the way down, how was he showing you up?

Helga Ah, well, you see I went down too far, and he had to show me up again.

Claude Oh, I see.

Karak scents a possible profit in this somewhere, and decides to play it carefully until the moment arrives for his kill

Karak Ja.

Helga Ja. Er . . .

There is a slight pause. Claude still looks puzzled, so Helga plunges on. Karak helps her by putting his hands up like reindeer antlers and treading with his foot

Yes—he was—er—telling me how he lost his herd.

Claude Lost his what?

Helga His herd of reindeer.

Claude *Reindeer?*

Helga Yes, and I said . . .

Karak (*pointedly*) Ja?

Helga I said—we would help to buy him some more.

Claude (*coldly*) Oh, did you?

Karak (*to Claude*) Ja. So you are please giving contribution to reindeer fund.

Claude (*pointedly*) I have a strong feeling I contributed earlier.

Karak Ja, but your wife is nice, kind lady. Is much nicer than other man's wife.

Claude (*taking out his wallet*) Oh, very well, here's ten francs.

Karak (*sternly*) Ten francs is not buying great, strong reindeer.

Claude Well, buy a small, sickly one and feed it up.

Karak Your wife is promising fifty francs.

Claude *Fifty francs?*

Karak Is nice, kind lady—is much nicer than——

Claude (*cutting in*) Oh, here you are.

Karak Thank you.

Karak grabs the money and goes to the camp-bed

Karak Merci bien, madame.

Karak exits to the bathroom with the camp-bed

Claude Really, darling. I can't see why you had to promise him fifty francs.

Helga Oh, but darling, I felt so sorry for him. You see all his reindeer died.

Claude But he's an hotel *porter*—not Father Christmas. What the hell does he want *reindeer* for?

Karak emerges from the bathroom and goes to the main door

Karak (*gravely*) Among my peoples reindeer is way of life. We are living off reindeer—we are milking reindeer, eating reindeer—wearing reindeer . . .
Claude Just where are you from?
Karak (*enjoying himself*) Mexico. (*He turns to go*)
Claude There aren't any reindeer in Mexico.

Karak turns. He has suddenly acquired a slight Mexican accent

Karak I know this, señor. (*He flaps the fifty-franc note at Claude*) Is reason I am saving up to buy some—buenas noches.

Karak exits

Claude (*furiously*) There you are, you see. He's a con-man. He's just conned us out of fifty francs.
Helga Oh, let's not argue, dear. It's your birthday.
Claude I was beginning to think it was *his* birthday.

Claude and Helga start to pull out the partition

Helga Tell me, how was your conference?
Claude Conference?
Helga I thought you came here for a conference.
Claude Oh, *that* conference. Yes. Oh, that was all right. Yes, fine.
Helga And what did you decide?
Claude Oh, nothing very much. We just conferred you know—as one does at conferences.
Helga Do you know this is the fourth conference you've attended in three weeks. Don't you ever decide anything?
Claude Yes, of course we did. We decided to hold another one next Friday.

Helga starts to unpack her suitcase. She takes out a pack of cards

Would you care to go out for a drink?
Helga Couldn't we have a drink up here?
Claude There's no room service. No, we'll have to go out.
Helga But I don't want to go out. I want to stay here with you.
Claude Yes—well, all right—but what are we going to do?
Helga We'll do what we always do. We'll have a nice game of cards. (*She starts to shuffle the cards*)

The main door opens and Stanley rushes in. He sits on Bed One, panting

Claude picks up the cards and starts playing

The main door opens and Simone enters

Stanley points to the partition and Simone lowers her voice

Simone Why did you run off and leave me? Just when they opened the bar again?

Stanley Ah, you see, that man was the Manager. He knows my wife.

Simone Oh, he wasn't looking at us, he was too busy arguing with those people. Who were they? (*She sits on the bed*)

Stanley Oh, those were the people he sent off to hospital.

Simone But there didn't seem much wrong with them.

Stanley Oh, there wasn't. That's why that man was trying to hit him.

Simone Well, if we can't go out, we might as well go to bed.

Stanley (*nervously*) What, now?

Simone Why not, darling? It's cabaret time.

Simone rises and switches on the transistor radio. Then she slowly begins to strip. On Bed Two, Helga and Claude hear the radio and put down their cards. Claude gets off the bed and goes into the main room. As he enters Simone starts gyrating to the music

Claude (*sternly*) What are you doing?

Simone We are going to bed, monsieur. Did you want something?

Claude (*conscious of Helga*) Bed? It's a little early to go to bed, isn't it?

Stanley decides to exact a little more revenge

Stanley Oh, not for us. No. (*He lies back on the bed*)

Simone No, it's my husband's favourite occupation.

Helga is listening to every word through the open partition door and Claude knows it. In the hope of delaying, if not preventing, the seduction of his mistress, he adopts a friendly tone

Claude Oh, is it? Well would you care to join my wife and me in a game?

Simone In a *game*, monsieur?

Claude Yes, we're playing on the bed, but if we all joined in, we could use that table.

Stanley How dare you!

Claude It's a game of *cards*. We often have a hand or two before we turn in. It relaxes us.

Stanley Well, we don't need relaxing, do we, darling?

Simone No, we have our own way of relaxing.

Simone starts her strip act. Claude swallows in anguish

Claude (*shouting*) Must you have that radio on?

Simone (*shouting*) Yes, we always undress to music, don't we, darling?

Stanley (*shouting*) Yes!

Simone starts removing her dress

Claude (*shouting*) Stop it!

Stanley (*shouting*) Stop what?

Claude (*shouting*) Stop everything! My wife has a headache.

Simone continues stripping. The music is now loud enough to provide a background to her act, but soft enough for the dialogue to be heard. Helga gets off the bed and comes into the main room. Simone is now cavorting in her black underwear. Helga looks at her and then at Claude. Helga is shocked

Helga Well, really, Claude!
Claude Oh, it's disgusting. I've told her to stop.
Helga They're married. What they do is their business.
Claude Well, we're married but we don't go on like that.
Helga It's none of your business what they do.
Claude But of course it is. They're in the same room.
Helga No they're not, they're in the room next door.
Claude Well there's only that partition. I mean it's like being in the same room.
Helga Oh, come out of it.

Helga pulls Claude into the Bed Two room and shuts the door. They sit on the bed and she picks up her cards. Claude reluctantly picks up his cards. Simone stops her act and turns to Stanley

Simone (*proudly*) How was that?
Stanley (*spellbound*) Incredible.

Simone slips on her dressing-gown

Simone Aren't you getting undressed, darling? (*She kneels on the bed*)
Stanley Oh no—I can't compete with you.

The idea appeals to Simone and she adopts a teasing manner

Simone Oh, let me see you try.
Stanley No.
Simone You want me to help you?
Stanley (*alarmed*) No!
Simone Well, get on with it. I'll give you an audition. You could earn lots on money in Paris.
Stanley I don't want to earn lots of money anywhere.
Simone (*coaxingly*) Oh, come on, darling, tease me a little.

She turns up the radio slightly, and sits on the bed. Stanley gets up rather uncertainly

You can't go to bed with your clothes on.

Stanley shamefacedly starts to remove his pullover. Simone gives sham cries of ecstasy

Oooh—that's right, darling. Ooooh!

Stanley takes his pullover off as Simone gives another loud moan of sham ecstasy. Claude hears this and looks at the partition door, then he looks at Helga, who is fixing him with a cold "just you try it" look

Ooooh, you are so sexy.

Stanley, uncertain whether he is being sent up, looks at her, but she appears to be in the throes of ecstasy. He starts to remove his trousers and then stops again

Ooooh, you are driving me mad, don't stop now.

Stanley shrugs and continues removing his trousers. Obviously there is no telling what pleases some women

Ooooh, keep going, darling, don't stop.

Claude gets off the bed, as Stanley starts slowly to remove his left sock, in a provocative way

Claude It's too much, it really is.
Helga Well you don't have to listen.
Claude I can't help listening.
Helga Plug your ears up.
Claude It's you I'm thinking about. I don't want you exposed to their animal behaviour. (*He makes a leap to the door*)
Helga (*shouting*) Claude!

Claude stops instantly

(*Sternly*) Come back here, don't you dare go out there!

In utter misery Claude goes back and sits on the bed. Stanley removes his right sock and waves it around his head

Simone (*ecstatically*) Oh, you are marvellous, darling, the best I have ever known.

Claude clasps his hands together and gives an agonized glance heavenwards. Stanley moves to the bathroom, waving his sock in the air. At the bathroom door he gives a sexy bump with his backside, which strains something

Holding his back, Stanley exits to the bathroom

Simone goes to the partition and listens. Claude gets off the bed and starts walking up and down

Claude Oh, it's disgusting, the way she's carrying on. Absolutely disgusting.
Helga Well, you don't have to go out and watch her.
Claude Ah yes—but what about his rash?
Helga Well, you won't cure his rash by watching her.
Claude No, no, no, my dear. I'm frightened he may *give* it to her.
Helga Well, if she doesn't mind getting it why are you worried?

Simone goes back to bed and starts fiddling with the radio

Claude (*in anguish*) Oh, but I am—I am. It could spread. We could *all* get it.
Helga I think that's rather unlikely.

On Bed One Simone gets the news in English on the radio

Voice on the Radio (*loudly*) —And here is the news in English.

Claude turns to the door and listens

   Stanley comes from the bathroom, in his pyjamas

Today the pound fell to its lowest ever rate on the foreign exchange market.

Claude listens at the partition door. Stanley is transfixed with alarm

British holidaymakers on the Continent were deeply shocked to find——

Simone twiddles the radio control, and gets a different programme

Different Radio Voice —Edmundo Ross in a bongo mood, with his maracas in Venezuela. (*And the radio goes into a South American melody*)

Claude looks puzzled, Stanley looks annoyed

Stanley (*shouting*) No, I want the other.

Stanley moves towards Simone on the bed. She playfully holds the radio away from him. He tries to grab it, and as she moves it further away he falls on the bed, and they go into what looks like a wrestling match for the radio, or a passionate struggle, depending on how you see it. Claude opens the partition door and takes the latter viewpoint. The radio goes off

   (*Shouting*) Let me have it—I *must* have it—I'm a British holidaymaker.
Claude (*losing control*) You're a filthy swine! Leave her alone.

Claude runs to the bed to drag Stanley off Simone and gets dragged into the struggle. Helga comes to the partition door, to see the three of them rolling on the bed

Helga Claude!

Claude takes no notice, he is trying to throttle Stanley and Simone is trying to drag him off. Helga runs to the bed and tries to grab Simone to pull her off Claude. But they all roll over and Helga gets dragged into the mêlée. The four of them are now rolling about on the bed

   The main door opens and Heinz enters. He carries the pike in one hand and a large handbell in the other. He freezes at what seems to be an orgy. Then rings his bell loudly

The group on the bed untangle themselves and sit up. Stanley stands up on the bed

Heinz (*coldly*) And what is the meaning of this?
Stanley Well, you see, we are British . . . and we're on holiday.
Heinz So it appears. (*He averts his shocked gaze from them*) I came to tell

you that the pageant is about to commence. And afterwards there will
be fireworks . . . *If* you are interested.

*Heinz exits, shutting the long feather in his cap in the top of the door.
They all watch as the feather slowly disappears*

Helga gets off the bed, and surveys the others coldly

Helga Really, Claude, would you mind explaining . . .?
Simone Yes. Are we to have no privacy?
Claude Well, we have to come in here to go to the bathroom.
Helga Oh, well perhaps it would be best if we had this room and they had
    that one.
Claude Why?
Helga So you can leave them alone.
Simone She is right. Come along, darling.

*Simone goes into the small room behind the partition. Helga goes to the
wardrobe and collects her coat*

Helga I need some fresh air.
Claude You go by all means.
Helga (*grimly*) Yes, and you are coming with me.
Claude Yes, dear.

*Helga throws Claude's coat at him. He catches it and glares at Stanley,
who is bouncing happily up and down on Bed One*

Helga Come along.
Stanley Bye-bye.

    Claude and Helga exit

*Stanley, smiling happily, gets off the bed and goes into the small room where
he sits on the end of the bed beside Simone*

Simone You know I think that shook him.
Stanley I don't know about him, but it certainly shook me.
Simone Well now.
Stanley Well now.

*Stanley, with high expectations, is waiting for Simone to make the next
move. Her attitude is somewhat ambiguous*

Simone We seem to be in a rather curious situation.
Stanley Oh, I wouldn't say that. No. We've told them we're married—I
    mean, we've got to go through with it.
Simone You mean you want to keep on pretending?
Stanley Oh, I think we ought to carry on for a bit.
Simone Carry on for a bit of what?
Stanley Well, we can't just stop now. Not after all the work we've put into it.
Simone But that was just to annoy Claude.

Stanley Well, I don't mind annoying him further. Come to that, I don't mind annoying him all night.

Simone So now you want to go to bed with me.

Stanley Oh, I didn't say that.

Simone Oh, you *don't* want to go to bed with me?

Stanley I didn't say that either.

Simone Why are you English such bloody hypocrites?

Stanley (*off guard*) I don't know—I think perhaps it's the weather.

Simone Well, I think—you are a worse hypocrite than Claude.

Stanley (*annoyed*) Oh, I like that. You're the one who started it. You said we had to go to bed together. You *blackmailed* me into agreeing.

Simone Did I, darling?

Stanley (*aggrieved*) Yes you did, and now when I'm ready you're trying to get out of it.

Simone I didn't say I was trying to get out of it.

Stanley Well, let's get into it. (*He starts to pull back the bed covers*)

Simone Not so fast. Earlier on you were worried about your conscience.

Stanley Well, that was earlier on. We've got a saying in England.

Simone What's that?

Stanley Never you mind.

Simone But you are forgetting one thing. I made a promise to myself, after tonight, I am finished with married men.

Stanley Yes, but that's *after*. Afterwards I think you should be. But not now.

Simone What about your wife?

Stanley She won't be back tonight.

Stanley leaps into bed. Simone has never made any indication whether or not she intends to join him, and at this point the main door opens

Brenda enters with Karak, who is carrying her suitcase. She has obviously been having words with him on the way up

Brenda Well I think it's disgraceful having to share the room.

Karak (*loudly*) Is no good blaming me. Is not my fault.

Brenda looks around the room. Stanley is frozen in horror. Simone can tell by looking at him what is wrong.

Simone (*pointing*) Your wife?

Stanley listens at the partition and nods

Brenda Where's my husband?

Karak Is probably in willage. Watching fireworks.

Brenda Oh yes, he would be. (*Pointing to the partition*) Who's in there?

Brenda goes to open the partition door. Before she reaches it, Simone rises and opens the door first. Stanley throws himself face down on the bed in an attempt to hide

Simone Madame. Do you mind? My babies are asleep.

Brenda Sorry, madame.

Simone closes the door and listens. She is joined by Stanley

(*To Karak*) How many have you put in here with us?

Karak (*cheerfully*) Who knows? Is dozens coming up here.

Brenda And where are we all sleeping?

Karak Is like barrack room. Always findink room for one more. (*He pats Bed One*) This bed is O.K. Is nobody sleepink in it.

Brenda Well no. Not at the moment.

Karak Then jump in quick and claim it. Before rest come back drunk and begin fighting.

Karak laughs. Brenda looks annoyed

Brenda I want to see the Manager. (*She goes to the bathroom with her case*)

Karak Manager is in willage. Dancing in fiesta. (*Karak goes to the door*) Sleep well, Nighty-night.

Karak exits with a cheerful wave through the main door. Brenda exits to the bathroom

Stanley (*in a panic*) What can we do?

Simone Just get dressed and go out there. Say—oh—say anything.

Stanley I can't. My clothes are in there.

Simone Now don't panic.

Stanley I am entitled to panic. That's my wife in there. She'll kill me.

Simone You could explain.

Stanley *Explain?* Explain what? Where do we *start*? You go out there, she doesn't know you. She won't suspect anything.

Simone Until *you* come out.

Stanley I'll stay in here.

Brenda comes out of the bathroom in her nightdress and gets into Bed One with a book

Simone And what happens when Claude and his wife come back?

Stanley That's it. I'm caught like a trap in a rat. What's she doing now?

Simone opens the door and peers out

Simone Good night.

Brenda Good night.

Simone shuts the door

Simone She's gone to bed with a book.

Stanley (*standing up on the bed*) That's it. She'll sit up all night reading. Waiting to pounce on me like a tiger. I'll have to get out of this window. I'll get out, and I'll go round—and I'll come up and I'll say I fell out the window sleepwalking.

Simone Oh, don't be so stupid. It's so simple. Your friend, Mrs Hoffmeyer.

Stanley What about her?

Simone (*pointing*) She's in there. Just knock on the door and go through.

Stanley No, I can't.

Simone Why? Have you quarrelled?

Stanley No. We haven't even *met*.

Simone But Claude said . . .

Stanley I don't care what Claude said. I do not know Mrs Hoffmeyer.

Simone Well, now is your chance to meet her.

Simone goes to the wallpapered door and bangs on it loudly

Stanley (*horrified*) What?

Simone (*calmly*) Look, just go in there, say you met her cousin in Budapest and he told you to look her up.

Stanley What, at midnight in my pyjamas?

Simone You never know your luck, chéri, she might be quite sexy. (*She bangs on the door again*) I don't think anybody is in there.

Stanley Well, that's it. The door's locked.

Simone bends down and peers through the keyhole. Brenda, in Bed One, is still sitting up in bed reading

Simone Ah, I think the key is in the keyhole. If it is—we may be lucky.

Stanley Oh, don't get her involved. I'll stay in here and I'll wait till Brenda goes to sleep and I'll creep in hoping the other two don't come back before I can get into the room . . . What are you doing?

During the above, Simone takes a magazine from the side of the bed, fiddles in her hair for a hairpin, takes one out and then, sliding the magazine under the door, pokes the hairpin in the keyhole

What are you doing?

Simone Using my ingenuity. (*She pulls the magazine back from under the door with a key on it*) Et voilà! We are in luck.

Stanley I wouldn't say that.

Simone puts the key in the door, and gently opens it, she peers into Mrs Hoffmeyer's room. Then she closes the door again

Anybody in there?

Simone There is an old girl in bed, I think she is asleep.

Stanley And supposing I wake her up?

Simone You won't wake her. She didn't wake when I knocked on the door, did she?

Stanley Well no, but . . .

Simone Just go through there and come back round and say you've been to the bathroom.

Stanley I've got a better idea. You go in there and I'll . . .

Simone Oh, don't argue with me. Just go.

Simone opens the door and pushes Stanley through, and then shuts the door

A moment's quiet and then suddenly, from Mrs Hoffmeyer's room, comes a loud awful series of screams and a loud crash as something heavy is knocked over. Simone freezes

Simone Oh—idiot!

The Lights fade to a Black-out. When they come up again, Brenda is in Bed One asleep. The light by her bed is out and she has the covers drawn over her face. The small room with Bed Two is empty. Simone and all her possessions have gone. Outside is heard the loud barking of dogs

The main door opens and Helga enters. Karak has opened the door with his pass-key. They talk in the doorway

Helga I'm sorry to bother you, but I lost my husband in the crowds, and he has the key.
Karak Is O.K. Is better I am showink you up here, with maniac loose in hotel.
Helga (*alarmed*) A maniac?
Karak Ja, maniac is attacking Mrs Hoffmeyer.
Helga Oh my God.
Karak Don't worry. Police is lookink for him—mit dogs.

Karak exits closing the door as the dogs bark furiously outside

Helga goes over to Bed One

Helga Claude . . .

Helga pulls the bedclothes back and sees it is a woman in bed, and a stranger. She looks puzzled, and then she goes over to the small bedroom and looks in. She sees it is empty, and goes in

Stanley enters through the wallpapered door. He is exhausted. He wears the monk's habit which has been burned off at the knees, under it his pyjama trousers have also been burned off. His face is blackened. He closes the door and leans against it.

Stanley Help me. Please help me.

Once again we hear the sound of dogs, and he clutches at Helga for protection. She pushes him away in sudden horror

Helga Are those dogs after *you*?
Stanley (*gasping*) After me? (*He turns and we see the backside is torn out of the monk's habit*) They *caught* me.
Helga Then you are the maniac who attacked Mrs Hoffmeyer . . . (*She points to the wallpapered door*)

Stanley (*gasping*) I didn't do anything. I didn't do anything at all. I went in there and fell over her bicycle. She saw me and screamed. I went down the fire escape—and she came after me. And then something terrible happened. And after that—I hid in the woods until I could get up here again.

He sinks down on the foot of Bed Two. Helga sits beside him

Helga (*pointing to the main room*) Who is that woman in there?
Stanley (*hesitantly*) That's my wife.
Helga Oh, I see. Then who was that other woman?
Stanley Oh, never mind—help me.
Helga Help you? Why should I help you?
Stanley Well, I helped you.

In despair he grovels at her feet and claws at her dress. She brushes him away

Helga But that was different. I was innocent.

Stanley clutches at her hands

Stanley (*imploringly*) But I am innocent. Oh, I am, I swear I'm innocent—innocent—I swear I haven't done anything.
Helga Don't lie to me. I saw you in there with her . . .
Stanley No you didn't.
Helga (*pushing him away*) Yes, and let go of my hand. I'm not your French girlfriend . . .
Stanley She is not *my* French girlfriend . . .

Helga looks at him, her suspicions now aroused

Helga Oh, then whose girlfriend is she?
Stanley (*hesitantly*) Nobody's.

Helga once more becomes the interrogator

Helga Now I want the truth, so don't lie to me. There are ways of finding out. Ja?
Stanley (*alarmed*) Ways? What sort of ways?
Helga Perhaps you would prefer talking to the police, ja?
Stanley No . . .
Helga Perhaps you won't get a chance to talk to them, perhaps the dogs will get you first, ja?
Stanley Nein . . . No.
Helga Then talk.
Stanley (*suddenly attacking back*) All right, I'll talk. I'll talk. I'll start with you going out the window on that rope.
Helga (*taken aback*) That has nothing to do with it.
Stanley Oh yes, it has. That's how it all started. That's why the dogs are after me. That's why they set fire to me . . .
Helga Who set fire to you?
Stanley Well, when I went down the fire escape, I was wearing my pyjamas,

and when I got down the bottom I found this monk's robe—the one you were wearing.

Helga So?

Stanley So I put it on and a whole crowd of people came towards me so I hid in this old cart full of firewood . . .

Helga Oh my God, they thought you were Saint Wolfgang.

Stanley Worse than that. They thought I was the dummy.

Helga Oh, but surely they could tell?

Stanley Yes, but it was too late. It was too late. Oh they tried to put the fire out—but they hadn't any water.

Helga Well, how did they put the fire out if they hadn't any water?

There is a pause

Stanley I'd rather not think about it.

Helga You are lucky to be alive.

Stanley They dragged me off, and they all patted me on the back and gave me drinks. Oh I was a right little village hero.

Helga Were you?

Stanley It didn't last, though.

Helga Why, what happened?

Stanley Mrs Hoffmeyer came up on her bicycle.

Helga She recognized you?

Stanley Recognized me! She smashed me on the head with her bicycle pump. (*He rubs his head*) The police came and the dogs—I ran away and hid in the woods until I could get up the fire escape again.

Helga becomes her usual efficient self

Helga Well, the first thing is to get rid of these clothes.

Stanley Hang on . . .

Without further ado, she yanks the monk's habit off him, as he struggles out of it

Helga Now your trousers . . .

Stanley (*protesting*) But I haven't anything underneath.

Helga Oh, don't argue with me, your trousers. Into bed—quick sharp . . .

Stanley gets under the bed cover

   That's it. Now.

She reaches under the cover and yanks his pyjama trousers off

Stanley Oh dear.

Helga lifts the cover up and looks under it

Helga Well, where is it?

Stanley I beg your pardon?

Helga I see no rash.

Stanley I haven't got one.

Helga opens the small window and drops out the robe and pyjama trousers

Helga No, and you never had one either.

Stanley No.

Helga (*turning on him*) And now the truth.

Stanley (*miserably*) Where do I start?

Helga Start with that woman you had in here.

Stanley Simone?

Helga Yes, she is Claude's girlfriend, isn't she?

Stanley (*hesitantly*) I don't know.

Helga Why are you protecting him?

Stanley I'm not . . . Well I am—'cause he—he said he'd tell Brenda about Gladys.

Helga (*intrigued*) Gladys? Now who's Gladys?

Stanley You are.

Helga Me?

Stanley Yes, when you went out of that window on that rope I said I had a girlfriend in here called Gladys.

Helga sits on the bed and looks at him. When she speaks again her manner is much softer

Helga Oh, I see, so you did all this to protect *me*. Yes?

Stanley I suppose I did. Yes.

Helga sits and looks at him as he stirs uneasily in bed

The main door opens and Claude creeps in

Brenda again has the covers over her head in Bed One. Claude thinks she is Helga. He takes his pyjamas from under the pillow

Claude (*whispering*) Helga? I'm sorry I was cross, Helga.

There is no answer

Claude exits to the bathroom

Helga stands up and looks at Stanley

Helga I am sorry I was cross with you just now.

Stanley Well, you weren't to know, were you?

Helga No, but when I think of what you have been through . . .

The romantic streak hidden behind Helga's cold front now starts emerging with a vengeance. It alarms Stanley more than the icy front

Stanley Yes, well, don't let's think about it.

Helga You did it all for my sake. You are a marvellous person, you really are.

Stanley No, I'm not.

Helga Oh yes, you are. No other man has ever done things like this for me—ever.

Stanley Yes, well, er . . .

Helga (*sitting beside him*) For you I would do anything. Anything you like.

Stanley Well, you don't have to do anything. Just don't tell Brenda—and keep Claude quiet.

At the mention of Claude, Helga becomes less romantic

Helga (*growing angry*) Claude, Claude—when I *think* of Claude.

Stanley (*anxiously*) Please don't cause a scene, you'll have the Manager up here—and those dogs.

Helga (*still angry*) Oh, don't worry. It's not England. They don't allow dogs in hotels.

Stanley Oh good. Do the dogs know?

Helga (*still angry*) Oh, Claude—the hypocrite! The two-faced, sanctimonious hypocrite! I'll *kill* him!

Stanley (*calming her*) Yes—do that—but wait till you get home—then you can do it quietly.

Helga Do what quietly?

Stanley Well, poison him, or suffocate him or anything you like.

Helga (*calmer*) Oh no, what is sauce for the gander is sauce for the goose.

Stanley Well, *goose* him—I don't care what you do but don't do it up here . . .

Helga (*thoughtfully*) But I am going to do it up here—and you're going to help me. Ja?

Helga kisses him. Then she moves away from the bed and starts to slowly undo the buttons on her dress

Stanley (*swallowing*) Help you?

Helga (*undoing more buttons*) Don't you want to?

Stanley I'd like to.

Helga Good.

Stanley I mean I'd like to *help* you . . .

Helga (*undressing further*) Good.

Stanley But I don't think I can.

Helga Why? Have you been helping somebody else?

Stanley No.

Helga (*undressing*) Are you sure?

Stanley Positive.

Helga No little French charities earlier on?

Stanley No.

Helga You know Claude says that I am not very sexy.

Stanley (*with feeling*) He must be raving mad.

Helga I was watching Simone getting ready for bed.

Stanley So I see.

Helga I don't like her, but I think perhaps I have learned something from her, ja?

Stanley Oh, you've cottoned on very sharpish.

Helga is now down to her bra and panties

Helga Well.

Stanley No. No. We ought to stop and think.

Helga Oh, don't worry; I've thought about it for ages. But with Claude, that's as far as it gets.

Stanley edges as far over in the bed as he can get and looks at her with a mixture of lust and apprehension. She gets into bed

Are you comfy?

Stanley Nicely, thank you.

Helga You know I am getting awfully fond of you.

Stanley Oh, I'm very fond of you, too.

Helga Do you remember earlier on, when you thought that I was the chambermaid . . .

Stanley Yes.

Helga (*leaning over towards him*) Do you still feel the same about me now?

Stanley Yes, but . . .

Helga But what?

Stanley My wife's in there . . .

Helga suddenly stops leaning over, and straightens up

Helga Oh my God, so she is—I had forgotten. I'm sorry.

Stanley No need to be sorry. (*He puts his arm around her shoulders*)

Helga But I am sorry. Because you're decent and you're nice—and you're married—and I'm behaving like a tart. (*She sniffs, on the verge of tears*)

Stanely No you're not.

Claude enters from the bathroom

Helga Yes I am. I'm horrible. I'm immoral. I'm cheap. I'm—I'm as bad as that Simone.

She starts to cry, which upsets Stanley. He moves towards her and tries to comfort her

Stanley Oh, please don't cry; please.

Helga Well, how would you feel if your wife was in bed with another man?

Claude gets into bed beside Brenda. Helga throws her arms round Stanley and sobs on his shoulder. Stanley pats her back. In Bed One Claude snuggles down into bed with his back to Brenda

Stanley There, there, there.

Helga (*sobbing*) It's just that Claude doesn't treat me like a woman. He turns his back on me.

Claude groans

Stanley Well, don't think about him.

Helga Oh, I can't help it. I mean, I've tried to be a good wife to him. I mean, I've tried to be affectionate.

Brenda turns in her sleep and throws an arm around Claude

I mean, I'm a normal woman with ordinary normal feelings.

Stanley (*comforting her*) Yes, of course. You're normal—very normal indeed.

Helga And so are you. Aren't you?

Stanley Oh yes. Yes, I am very normal . . .

Helga suddenly moves away from him

Helga No . . .

Stanley What's the matter now?

Helga Your wife is in there.

Stanley Yes, but I've just remembered about the business with her and the hotel manager.

Helga How long have you been married?

Stanley (*dazed*) Nine years. How long have you?

Helga (*dazed*) Ten.

Stanley (*dazed*) Nine and ten is nineteen. We've been married nineteen years.

Helga (*dazed*) Have we really, darling? It doesn't seem that long.

And they go into a passionate embrace

Stanley Oh Helga.

Claude (*in his sleep*) Helga.

Stanley (*passionately*) Oh Helga, Helga, Helga.

Claude (*in his sleep*) Oh Helga, Helga, Helga. (*He turns in bed and embraces Brenda*)

Stanley Helga . . .

Brenda suddenly wakes up and realizes the man embracing her isn't Stanley

Brenda (*screaming*) Help! Help . . .!

Claude struggles out of bed and stands looking at her, frozen in horror. Helga and Stanley break off their embrace at the same time, and Helga leaps out of bed, snatching her dress, and slips it on, she starts buttoning it up frantically

Helga What's the matter with her?

Helga is once again crisp and efficient. She opens the door and peers out and then relaxes. She shuts the door and turns to Stanley, smiling. In Bed One Brenda is sitting with the bedclothes pulled up around her while Claude stands in an attitude of horror, opening and closing his mouth wordlessly

Helga It's Claude. He tried to get in bed with your wife.

Stanley (*not amused*) Why, I'll kill him. Get my trousers.

The main door bursts open and Heinz enters, carrying his pike

Heinz Somebody was screaming in here, I think.
Brenda (*pointing*) That man, he attacked me. He got in bed with me.

Heinz lowers his pike and presses it against Claude, who retreats and puts his hands up in surrender

Heinz So you are the maniac.

Helga is at the partition door listening. Stanley joins her, wrapped in a bed sheet

Claude What do you mean—it was all a mistake.
Heinz (*screaming*) A mistake? You ravish Mrs Hoffmeyer. You have my hotel struck off her list, before it is even on.

Heinz backs Claude into the armchair and Claude holds the end of the pike which is at his chest

Claude I don't know what you're talking about.
Heinz (*raising the pike for a thrust*) Silence, you schweinhund! You rapist! Through you we have lost the lady Bulgarian bicycle riders for ever.

Karak enters, sums up the situation and hurries forward to prevent Claude's murder

Heinz is about to skewer Claude with the pike

Karak Lunatic. What are you doink?
Heinz I'm killing this rapist.
Karak (*grabbing the pike*) You are mad.
Heinz (*sobbing in fury*) But you don't know what he has done to me.
Karak He is raping *you* as well?
Heinz Worse. He has raped my hotel. And my aunt . . .
Karak Nobody *raped* your aunt. It wasn't necessary.
Claude (*bewildered*) I haven't raped anyone. I don't even know his aunt— unless that's her. (*He indicates Brenda*)
Heinz Silence.

As Karak held the pike, Claude managed to rise from the chair and move slightly away from it. Heinz now charges at Claude with the pike, but Karak has taken a firm hold of it and Heinz runs forward leaving it in Karak's hands. He skids to a halt

Karak Now listen, before you are killing him. First he must be identified by Mrs Hoffmeyer.
Heinz Why?
Karak Is correct procedure in rape cases. (*With feeling*) Believe me—*I* am knowink.
Heinz Very well then, take him to her.

Karak hands the pike to Heinz, who rejects it

Karak You will need it—in case he escapes.

Karak pushes the pike back to Heinz

If he try to escape—I break his neck mit karate chop.

With a terrible snarl Karak makes a karate-chop movement at Claude, who flinches

Claude Oh, I shan't—I promise you.

> *With Karak behind him, arm raised ready for a death blow, Claude exits. Karak follows*

Heinz puts the pike up against the chair and goes to Bed One. He puts one knee on the bed and extends a hand to Brenda, who is standing on the bed with the bedclothes round her and looking at him in admiration

Heinz (*suddenly suave*) My dear lady. It was not what he did to my hotel which angered me. It was the thought of him attacking you.
Stanley (*alarmed*) Get my clothes—quick!

Helga goes through the door into the main room and picks up Stanley's clothes from the side of the bed where he left them during his strip. Brenda and Heinz turn to look at her

Helga (*coldly*) My husband and I are leaving.

Helga returns to the partition door with the clothes. Heinz follows her

Heinz Your husband is certainly leaving. Of this I can assure you.
Helga Oh yes?

Helga slams the partition door in Heinz's face. Stanley is holding up the bedcover in front of himself. Helga takes the bedcover and holds it in front of him while he dresses behind it, then listens at the door

Brenda Is that his wife?
Heinz Yes.
Brenda (*with a sudden thought*) You mean he is staying in this room, too?

Heinz leads Brenda to the pouffe and seats her. He stands beside her. She still retains the bedcover, holding it around her modestly

Heinz Oh yes—but that is no excuse.
Brenda But perhaps he got in the wrong bed.
Heinz With Mrs Hoffmeyer? She is next door.
Brenda Oh—of *course*. I wonder where my husband is?
Heinz He should be here protecting you. If I was your husband—I would never let you out of my sight.
Brenda (*impressed by his ardour*) But then you're not, are you?

Heinz sighs deeply and presses her hand to his lips

Oh, but you won't go till he comes back, will you?
Heinz Of course not. My dear—Brenda . . . (*He sits beside her on the pouffe*)

Brenda (*surprised and pleased*) How do you know my name?
Heinz I heard your husband calling you. When you were in the bathroom.
Brenda But I haven't been in the bathroom. I've been driving round all night looking for that ring.
Heinz Did you find it?
Brenda (*sniffing*) No.
Heinz You know, Karak found a ring earlier in the car-park.
Brenda What's it like?
Heinz I don't know. I think he is trying to keep it—but don't worry—we shall ask him for it when he comes back.
Brenda Yes.
Heinz (*leaning towards her*) You know you are very lovely.

Brenda rises but does not move very far

Brenda No. My husband . . .
Heinz Should be here protecting you—as I am protecting you.

Heinz drags the bedcover off Brenda, takes her hand, then pulls her down on to his knee

Brenda Ooooh!

Heinz sweeps Brenda backwards and kisses her. Helga is still listening at the door. Stanley is now dressed. She opens the door and peers out

Helga (*whispering*) Now.

Helga stands aside and Stanley goes through it, and runs towards the main door, going over Bed One in his journey. Heinz is still in a passionate embrace with Brenda. Stanley gets to the main door. bangs it twice as if he had just entered, and then stands with a look of outraged horror. Brenda and Heinz rise, shocked

Stanley (*hollowly*) Brenda—oh Brenda. (*He looks and sounds like a man whose world is suddenly shattered*)
Brenda It wasn't my fault, Stanley. You should have been here.
Heinz Now I can explain all this.
Stanley (*grimly*) Can you . . .?
Heinz (*moving towards his pike*) Given time—yes.
Stanley (*grimly*) I'm afraid that for you—time is running out.

Stanley grabs the pike before Heinz can reach it. He now menaces Heinz with it, and Heinz retreats until he is at the pouffe. He falls backwards over it, and Stanley raises the pike and pins him to the pouffe

Brenda (*alarmed*) Stanley—don't do anything silly.
Heinz Please—this costume is only borrowed.

Karak enters, followed by Claude

Karak Hey, what are you doing?

Karak walks over calmly

Stanley Thank God you stopped me in time.

Stanley hands the pike to Karak. Heinz struggles to his feet, and points to Claude

Heinz Has Mrs Hoffmeyer identified that criminal?
Claude No—she established my complete innocence.
Heinz Ja—and she is leavink hotel rightaway . . .

There is a loud clatter like the sound of a bicycle falling over. Karak hurries back to the open door

Karak All right, madame, I am helping mit bicycle.

Karak exits

Claude (*turning on Heinz*) As for you, sir, I shall sue you. And further-more, I shall demand . . .

Claude falters to a halt as Helga, fully dressed and carrying her suitcase, emerges from behind the partition

Helga Oh yes, Claude—what will you do?

At the same time, Simone enters from the bathroom, dressed as a nun

Simone Peace be with you.
Heinz (*seeing Simone*) Who is that nun?
Simone (*saintly*) Oh, I am just passing through on my way to the convent. I shan't be stopping. I have so many little charities to attend to. (*She raises her hand in benediction*) Bless you, my children, and try to behave better in future.

Simone moves to the door and turns, there is no back to her robe, which displays her underwear. She pauses at the door and gives a bump with her backside, then exits

Heinz (*astounded*) But who is she? Where did she come from?
Helga (*sweetly*) Perhaps my husband can explain—Claude?
Claude I thought she was with him. (*He indicates Stanley*)
Brenda Stanley?
Stanley I have never seen that woman before in my life.

Karak runs in

Karak (*excitedly*) I have just seen nun mit bare bum.
Heinz Karak—the ring you found.

Karak brings his hand up. He is now wearing the signet ring

Karak Oh, you are meanink this?
Brenda Let me see that ring. (*Recognizing it*) Yes, that's it, that's mine.

Karak (*astounded*) Yours?

Stanley What are you doing with my wife's ring?

Karak (*to Brenda*) Where are you getting it from?

Brenda My father gave it to my mother just before he went off in the war.

Karak No, no is not possible . . . Yes—now I am seeink family likeness. (*He suddenly sweeps up Brenda in his arms and swings her in a fatherly embrace*)

Stanley Put my wife down.

Heinz Karak, have you gone completely insane?

Karak Brendushka—my little Brendushka—Daddy is back.

Stanley (*in horror*) Oh no—no—please no—no . . .

Karak releases Brenda and turns on Stanley

Karak Ja, I am marrying her mother at Stoke-on-Trent during the war. (*He starts to chase Stanley*) And you—you are son-in-law.

Stanley (*retreating*) No—Brenda—get packed, we're leaving.

Karak (*kissing Stanley on both cheeks*) Yes, we are leavink. I am comink to live mit you in England.

Stanley (*screaming*) No. Oh no . . . (*He staggers to the pouffe and sinks down on it*)

More or less simultaneously, Heinz rushes forward and shakes Brenda by the hand and Helga takes her other hand and presses it

Helga How marvellous to find your father like this.

Heinz Of course he must live with you. I insist.

Claude (*shaking Stanley's hand*) Congratulations, my dear fellow.

Helga and Brenda are grouped by Stanley at the pouffe

Brenda Daddy can help you do out the bathroom.

Stanley (*babbling dementedly*) No, no, no, no, no . . .

Heinz (*shaking Karak's hand*) Good-bye, Karak.

Stanley No, no . . .

Karak picks up the bottle of cognac from the table and raises it in a toast before drinking out of it

Karak To my new family.

Stanley Oh no—I knew it. I knew it. I knew it.

Brenda Knew what?

Stanley I knew we should have gone to Skegness.

Brenda and Helga both kiss Stanley as—

the CURTAIN *falls*

FURNITURE AND PROPERTY LIST

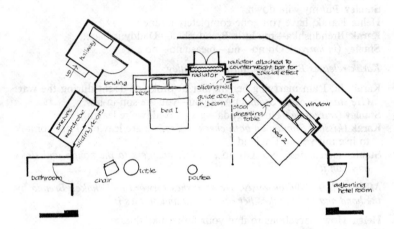

ACT I

On stage: 2 double beds with bedding
   Dressing-table. *On it:* telephone, 2 foreign magazines. *In drawer:* box
       of tissues, 2 hand-mirrors
   Stool
   Bedside table. *On it:* lamp
   Occasional table
   Armchair
   Pouffe
   Fitted wardrobe with 2 sliding doors
   Radiator
   On wall: cuckoo clock
   On windowsill behind radiator: spanner
   Carpet
   Window curtains

Off stage: Toolbag with hammer, spanner, saw, can of beer, 2 screwdrivers
       (Karak)
   Festival poster, pamphlets **(Heinz)**
   Torch **(Brenda)**
   Plastic shopping-bag with *Woman* magazine, tow-rope, fly-spray,
       Stanley's slippers **(Brenda)**

Suitcase **(Brenda**'s) with toilet-bag, make-up, hand-lotion, dressing **(Heinz)**
Suitcase **(Stanley's)** with toilet-bag, towel, cognac bottle, trousers, pullover, dressing **(Heinz)**
Suitcase **(Helga's)**, unopened **(Karak)**
Vanity-case **(Helga's)** with dress in dry-cleaner's bag, slippers, dressing-gown, toilet-bag, pack of cards **(Karak)**
Holdall **(Karak)**
Suit in plastic cover **(Karak)**
Lavatory chain **(Claude)**
Pike with decorative ribbons **(Heinz)**
Tray with bottle of Scotch and 2 glasses **(Karak)**

Personal: **Heinz:** rose
Brenda: engagement ring
Helga: coins in handbag
Karak: chewing-gum
Claude: wallet full of franc notes, coins

ACT II

Strike: Tow-rope, chain, pamphlets, plastic suit-bag, *Woman* magazine, **Stanley's** coat and shoes

Set: Both beds tidy
Claude's pyjamas under pillow of Bed Two
Claude's slippers under chair
Stanley's suitcase in wardrobe
Cognac bottle in **Stanley's** suitcase
Claude's holdall in wardrobe
Simone's case open on Bed One. *In it:* corset, suspender-belt, nylons, nun's outfit, dressing-gown, transistor radio
Simone's hat, jewel case with bracelet, and powder compact on Bed One
Simone's coat on pouffe
French magazine on floor by wallpapered door

stage: Camp-bed **(Karak)**
Handbell **(Heinz)**
Paperback book **(Brenda)**
Key (Stage Management—for **Simone)**
Pass-key **(Karak)**

Personal: **Heinz:** lace handkerchief
Karak: ring

LIGHTING PLOT

Property fittings required: wall brackets, table lamp, trick wall bed lamp above
    Bed Two
A bedroom. The same scene throughout

ACT I. Night

To open: Wall brackets on, table lamp on, wall bed lamp off

Cue 1	**Karak** switches on light *Shower of sparks from wall bed lamp*	(Page 4)
Cue 2	**Karak:** "Is working." *All lights dim, then out*	(Page 4)
Cue 3	**Stanley** falls downstairs *Lights up as before*	(Page 5)

ACT II. Night

To open: As close of previous act

Cue 4	**Simone:** "Oh—idiot!" *Black-out*	(Page 70)
Cue 5	When ready *Return to previous lighting, but with Bed One table lamp off*	(Page 70)

EFFECTS PLOT

ACT I

Cue 1   **Karak** drinks beer   **(Page 1)**
Telephone rings

Cue 2   **Karak:** "... full of woodworm."   **(Page 2)**
Cuckoo clock strikes

Cue 3   **Heinz:** "... woodworm do not eat plastic."   **(Page 2)**
Radiator gives three bangs

Cue 4   **Karak:** "... death watch beetle."   **(Page 3)**
Radiator bangs

Cue 5   **Brenda:** "... come back *down* a flight."   **(Page 5)**
Crash of someone falling downstairs

Cue 6   **Heinz:** "... but it's nothing."   **(Page 6)**
Ambulance siren approaches

Cue 7   **Heinz:** "... I must go."   **(Page 6)**
Second ambulance siren approaches

Cue 8   **Stanley:** "It's freezing."   **(Page 7)**
Ambulance sirens start up and fade

Cue 9   **Stanley** turns radiator tap   **(Page 13)**
Radiator bangs

Cue 10   **Stanley** turns off radiator with spanner   **(Page 21)**
Radiator bangs and cloud of steam escapes

Cue 11   **Helga:** "Yes, you were."   **(Pa** 2 **?)**
Radiator bangs twice

Cue 12   **Stanley** slips trousers down   **(Page 24)**
Cuckoo clock strikes

Cue 13   As radiator reaches ceiling   **(Page 38)**
Steam effect from radiator

Cue 14   **Stanley:** "... put these on."   **(Page 38)**
Brass band approaches, passes, and fades

ACT II

Cue 15   **Simone** switches on transistor radio   **(Page 45)**
Tyrolean music—continuing until **Simone** *exits*

Cue 16   **Simone** switches on transistor radio   **(Page 62)**
"Strip" music

MADE AND PRINTED IN GREAT BRITAIN BY
LATIMER TREND & COMPANY LTD PLYMOUTH

MADE IN ENGLAND